MW01290661

A Bible-Based Chronology from the Creation to the Second Advent of Jesus Christ

Jim Dodge

WESTBOW
PRESS®
A DIVISION OF THOMAS NELSON
& ZONDERVAN

THE HOLY BIBLE, NEW INTERNATIONAL VERSION®, NIV® Copyright © 1973, 1978, 1984, 2011 by Biblica, Inc.® Used by permission. All rights reserved worldwide.

Scripture taken from the King James Version of the Bible.

Scripture quotations marked (NLT) are taken from the Holy Bible, New Living Translation, copyright © 1996, 2004, 2007 by Tyndale House Foundation. Used by permission of Tyndale House Publishers, Inc., Carol Stream, Illinois 60188. All rights reserved.

WestBow Press books may be ordered through booksellers or by contacting:

WestBow Press
A Division of Thomas Nelson & Zondervan
1663 Liberty Drive
Bloomington, IN 47403
www.westbowpress.com
1 (866) 928-1240

Because of the dynamic nature of the Internet, any web addresses or links contained in this book may have changed since publication and may no longer be valid. The views expressed in this work are solely those of the author and do not necessarily reflect the views of the publisher, and the publisher hereby disclaims any responsibility for them.

Any people depicted in stock imagery provided by Getty Images are models, and such images are being used for illustrative purposes only. Certain stock imagery © Getty Images.

ISBN: 978-1-9736-4359-3 (sc)
ISBN: 978-1-9736-4360-9 (hc)
ISBN: 978-1-9736-4358-6 (e)

Library of Congress Control Number: 2018912881

Print information available on the last page.

WestBow Press rev. date: 11/8/2018

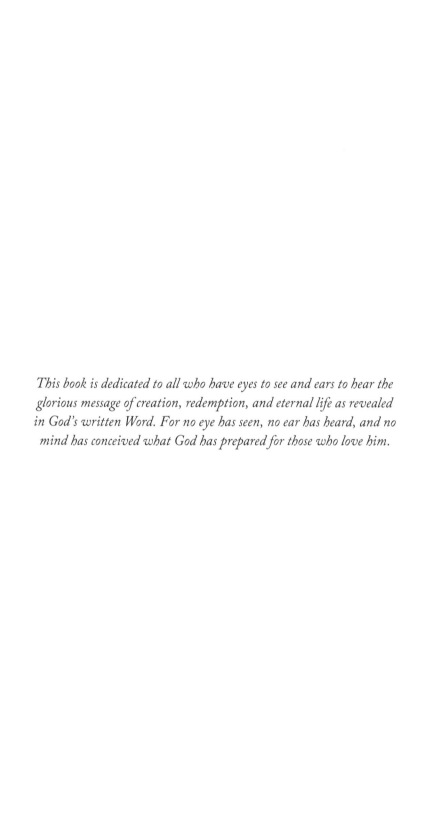

This book is dedicated to all who have eyes to see and ears to hear the glorious message of creation, redemption, and eternal life as revealed in God's written Word. For no eye has seen, no ear has heard, and no mind has conceived what God has prepared for those who love him.

CONTENTS

INTRODUCTION

This book has been written to inspire and strengthen the faith of true Christian believers for today, in these latter days, who earnestly await the return of our blessed hope, the Lord Jesus Christ. It is intended to be a blessing for all who continue to hold the Bible to be the divinely inspired, incomparable, infallible, inerrant Word of God. The Scriptures reveal that the latter days will be characterized by an increasingly chaotic world of godlessness and lawlessness, where:

1. God's Word will be neglected as the supreme authority for faith and practice.
2. Scripture is twisted, distorted, and spiritualized for self-serving agendas. Truth has become subjective and relative.
3. Entertainment, idolatry, liturgy, and rituals have replaced the Lord Jesus from being the central focus of worship in mainline churches. Apostasy will increase.
4. Teaching has become heavily influenced by false doctrines. Jesus has been removed from the public square and is now being removed from the Church.
5. The average (casual or cultural) Christian is ignorant or has become apathetic about many, if not most, foundational biblical doctrines, especially those concerning the Creation, Bible prophecy, and the Second Coming. There will be a great falling away from the faith.

The Word of God, with its incredible message of creation, redemption, and eternal life, has always been under attack by the secular world, and so it should not be a surprise to see what's happening in the world—and now in the Church. The good news is that God's Word never changes: "Forever, O Lord, thy word is settled in heaven" (Ps 119:86). Importantly, for these end-times, the Bible contains an amazingly accurate timeline (chronology) dating from the Creation to the Second Coming, even though it has been intentionally hidden and is only revealed in these latter days, exactly as the prophet Daniel was told more than 2,500 years ago: "But thou, O Daniel, shut up the words and seal the book, even to the time of the end: many shall run to and fro, and knowledge shall be increased" (Daniel 12:4).

This Bible-based chronology relies on a literal interpretation of the Scriptures. It involves three absolute dates, none of which were known or could be understood until the mid-twentieth century when advances in technology led to increased knowledge and illumination about these long hidden, or not understood, Bible secrets. The chronology spans more than six thousand years of history, from the six-day Creation in the Old Testament to the earthly life and ministry of Jesus Christ (the First Advent), and to the climax of God's plan, the Second Advent of Christ. The presently unfolding end-time chronology is revealed in chapter 6 and describes specific windows of time that highlight the latter days, the season of the Lord's return, and a specific generation that will "see all these things" before it passes away so that we, as children of light, should not let the day of the Lord's return overtake us as a thief in the night.

I pray that this book will inspire confidence in the holy Scriptures and the signs, numbers, days, and years revealed in them about God's chronological timeline of history, and that it will honor and glorify our Lord of creation and salvation, Jesus Christ.

PREFACE

But thou, O Daniel, shut up the words, and seal the book, even to the time of the end: many shall run to and fro, and *knowledge shall be increased.* (Daniel 12:4; emphasis added)

In the fall of 2017, while pondering the breathtaking pace of prophetic events and what clearly seemed to be a convergence of signs for the time of the end or latter days happening, I was drawn to Daniel 12:4. In the passage, the angel of the Lord told Daniel to seal up the books until the "time of the end," when knowledge will increase. Nearly six hundred years after Daniel, in his letter to the Thessalonians, Paul tells us, "But of the times and seasons, brethren, ye have no need that I write unto you, for yourselves know perfectly that the day of the Lord so cometh as a thief in the night ... But ye brethren are not in darkness that *that day should overtake you* like a thief (1 Thessalonians 5:1–2, 4; emphasis added).

Both the prophet and the apostle were revealing that as the time of the end draws near, God will begin to unseal the book revealed to Daniel (Daniel 12:9) and knowledge will increase so that believers will (or at least should) become aware and prepare for what is coming. Although the Scriptures provide a fairly precise chronology and timeline for the events involved in the seven-year period known as Daniel's seventieth week, I wondered what illumination our "increased knowledge" might reveal today about the chronology of end-time events in the times when the prophecies are being fulfilled.

Then an even more compelling question came to mind. In this age of increased knowledge prophesied by Daniel, do we now have the tools and wisdom to compile a complete and accurate Bible chronology dating from the Creation to the time, or at least the "season," of the Lord's return? From my research on the Christmas star, I knew that although the Scriptures reveal thousands of years of history dating from the Creation, there are apparent gaps, questions, uncertainties, and even conflicts involving historical issues that have prevented the compilation of a truly accurate timeline for God's plan, especially one that links the three main periods of Bible history—the Old Testament, the New Testament, and the Second Coming—together as a continuous, unbroken timeline. Thus, an objective in this book was to make a concerted effort to bring these three main segments of history together based as much as possible on the Scriptures, using tools and resources that have only become available in the last century in order to confirm whether or not the period of the end-times has indeed been hidden from our eyes until now, just as Daniel prophesied more than 2,500 years ago.

My primary resource was *The New Defender's Study Bible (KJV)* by Dr. Henry M. Morris (1995). In his introduction, Dr. Morris has this to say about his approach to the Bible.

> The Bible does contain many teachings that Christians have disagreed about, of course, and some annotated Bibles try to take neutral positions on such controversial doctrines. I have thought it best, however, to express my own convictions on these matters, even at the risk of losing readers who hold to other views ... Thus, a literal approach has been taken, not only in Genesis, but throughout the whole Bible.[1]

Dr. Morris's notes, annotations, comments, and appendices were invaluable and insightful, and they contributed mightily to this effort. It was the primary resource used to develop the chronology in chapters 1 and 2, which dated people and events starting from the creation year. Scriptures cited in this book are from the King James Version of the Bible unless otherwise noted.

A second resource critical to resolving the Old Testament chronology was *The Mysterious Numbers of the Hebrew Kings* by Dr. Edwin R. Thiele (1951). Although the Scriptures are filled with chronological data for the period of the Hebrew kings and divided kingdom, dating for this period was difficult, if not impossible, to harmonize between Israel and Judah and between the two kingdoms and their neighbors. Chapter 3 describes how the seemingly irreconcilable differences in the chronologies of the Hebrew kings were resolved to support a literal interpretation of the Scriptures. Though resolution of the chronologies for the Hebrew kings was important, Dr. Thiele's most critical contributions to this effort were: (1) the determination of an "absolute date" that linked together the chronologies, dating backward from the modern era and forward from creation, and (2) the inclusion of an accurate chronology for the Persian kings in his book.

Because Daniel's seventy-week prophecy is the only passage in Scripture that contains chronological data that seems to link the post-exile period of Judah with the life and ministry of Jesus Christ, chapter 4 addresses the period between the decree of Persian king Artaxerxes to rebuild Jerusalem and Christ's First Coming. It may be controversial. Like many Christians, I once believed Sir Robert Anderson's claims in *The Coming Prince* (1894), based on twelve thirty-day months equating to a 360-day "prophetic year." Anderson made four claims in his book using prophetic year reckoning that are addressed in chapter 4. This chapter is important because Anderson appears to rely on the Scriptures to make his case. Even so, I conclude that Anderson's prophetic year reckoning is incorrect and is not supported by Scripture.

Fortunately, God does not depend on the calendars or chronologies of man to reveal His truth. This is especially true for the most significant event in history: the first advent of His Son, Jesus Christ. Chapter 5 focuses on what the Scriptures tell us about the chronology revealed in God's heavenly signs. The heavens provide the only dating system that can reveal events from history past (and in the modern era, for history future) with precision, to an exact date, time, and location anywhere on earth. In chapter 5, the astronomical tools and resources used to develop the Christmas star timeline have been employed to scripturally support a literal interpretation of the Nativity story that dates the birth of Christ at June 17, 2 BC, resulting in a Scripture-based chronology for the life and ministry of Jesus.

Chapter 6 is the final and most important chapter for Christians today because the events it describes have not yet happened. The chronology defined for this period, labeled the latter days, is based on the most accurate chronological resource of all: the very words of Jesus Christ Himself! At the end of His earthly ministry, the disciples asked Him, "When will all these things happen?" (Matthew 24:3). In his answer, Jesus gave a detailed description of what to expect, and He provided two precisely sequenced windows of time that provide great insight about the timing of latter day critical events. Not surprisingly, Christ's words are supported by incredible revelations from the Old Testament that have been known for centuries but that are only now beginning to be understood.

It is hoped that truths revealed in this Bible-based chronology will increase the faith of Christians in a literal interpretation of the Scriptures, that it will make them aware of the prophetic times we are in today, and that it helps to prepare every believer for the soon return of our blessed hope, the Lord and Savior Jesus Christ.

CHAPTER 1

BIBLICAL CHRONOLOGY OF THE PATRIARCHS FROM THE CREATION TO JACOB

In the beginning, God created.
—Genesis 1:1

The chronology developed in this book is Bible based, and therefore it begins at the beginning when God created everything in six literal days. That was only thousands—not billions—of years ago, according to the Bible. This may be difficult for many to believe at a time when the "fact" of evolution has been taught in the American public education as the only acceptable answer to the question of origins for more than fifty years. It should hardly be surprising that attacks on the Bible today have been greatest and most focused on the integrity and authority of Genesis in particular because evolutionism (the assumption that our complex universe can somehow be explained without God in the picture) is the only alternative to the creation narrative. Nevertheless, to be Bible based, as the title of this book indicates, the chronology herein necessarily starts with the creation account as revealed in Genesis. There are two reasons: the doctrine of creation clearly pervades the rest of the Bible, and there is not a hint of evolutionism to be found anywhere in scripture.

Although the issue of origins is not a purpose of this book, a review of critical Old Testament and New Testament passages that confirm and reaffirm the creation narrative as laid out in Genesis is provided for the reader in Appendix 1. If you have doubts or questions or simply don't know what the Bible says about this important foundational doctrine, please take time to review Appendix 1 before continuing. It may provide illumination and become a valuable source of increased faith in God's holy Word.

Let us begin.

The Bible chronology, dating from the Creation (from Adam to Jacob), is fairly straightforward. It comes directly from the genealogies of the patriarchs in Genesis 5 and 11 and as confirmed in 1 Chronicles 1. With the starting point of the creation as the year 0, the patriarchs are listed in sequence with each one's age at the birth of his succeeding son and his age at death. For example, Adam bore Seth when he was 130 years old (130 years after the creation), Adam died at the age of 930 (930 years after the creation), and so on. This biblically established chronology from the genealogies of the patriarchs continues from the creation of Adam to the death of Jacob. The table below for the twenty-two generations from Adam to Jacob has been reproduced from Appendix 10, "Chronology of the Patriarchs from Genesis," in the *New Defenders Study Bible* by Dr. Henry M. Morris.[1] In the columns, the letters "AC" indicate the years after the Creation. Thus, Adam died in the year 930 AC, Seth was born in the year 130 AC, and Jacob died in 2255 AC. The scripture references from Genesis and 1 Chronicles have been added in the left column of the table.

Table 1: Chronology of the Patriarchs from Genesis 5 and 11

Name	Year of Birth After Creation	Age at birth Of Son	Age at Death	Year of Death After Creation	Bible References
Adam	0*	130	930	930 AC	Gen 5:3-5; 1 Ch 1:1
Seth	130 AC	105	912	1042 AC	Gen 5:6-8; 1 Ch 1:1
Enos	235 AC	90	905	1140 AC	Gen 5:9-11; 1 Ch 1:1
Cainan	325 AC	70	910	1235 AC	Gen 5:12-14, 1 Ch 1:2
Mahalaleel	395 AC	65	895	1290 AC	Gen 5:15-17; 1 Ch 1:2
Jared	460 AC	162	962	1422 AC	Gen 5:18-20; 1 Ch 1:2
Enoch	622 AC	65	365**	987 AC	Gen 5:21-24; 1 Ch 1:3
Methuselah	687 AC	187	969	1656 AC	Gen 5:25-27; 1 Ch 1:3
Lamech	874 AC	182	777	1651 AC	Gen 5:28-31; 1 Ch 1:3
Noah	1056 AC	502	950	2006 AC	Gen 5:32,9:28-9; 1 Ch 1:4
Shem	1558 AC	100	600	2158 AC	Gen 11:10-11; 1 Ch 1:4
Arphaxad	1658 AC	58	438	2096 AC	Gen 11:12-13; 1 Ch 1:17-18
Salah	1693 AC	30	433	2126 AC	Gen 11:13-15; 1 Ch 1:18-19
Eber	1723 AC	34	464	2187 AC	Gen 11:14,16-17;1 Ch 1:19,25
Peleg	1757 AC	30	239	1996 AC	Gen 11:16-19; 1 Ch 1:19,25
Reu	1787AC	32	239	2026 AC	Gen 11:18-21; 1 Ch 1:25
Sarug	1819 AC	30	230	2049 AC	Gen 11:20-23; 1Ch 1:26
Nahor	1849 AC	29	148	1997 AC	Gen 11:22-25; 1Ch 1:26

Terah	1878 AC	70	205	2083 AC	Gen 11:24-27,32 1Ch 1:26
Abraham	1948 AC	100	175	2123 AC	Ge 11:26-7,21:5, 25:7,1 Ch 1:28
Isaac	2048 AC	60	180	2228 AC	Ge 21:5, 25:26,35:28; 1 Ch 1:28
Jacob	2108 AC	---	137	2255 AC	Gen 25:26, 47:28; 1 Ch 1:34

* Adam was created as an adult on the sixth day of creation.
** Enoch's age at the time he was translated and the time of his translation.

Notes

1. The table assumes no gaps in the lists in Genesis 5 and 11, as confirmed by 1 Chronicles 1.
2. Adam could have known all the preflood patriarchs except Noah and Shem.
3. Noah could have known all the preflood patriarchs except Adam and Seth.
4. Noah and Shem could have known Abraham.
5. Shem could have known Isaac and Jacob.

From this table and the scriptures, other major events during the first two millennia after the Creation can be determined. For example, Genesis 7:6 tells us that the flood occurred in the six hundredth year of Noah. Noah was born in 1056 AC, and thus his 600th year, the year of the flood, was 1656 AC. This is the same year that Noah's grandfather, Methuselah, died at the age of 969. We can determine that Abraham was born 292 years (1948 - 1656 = 292) after the flood. The scriptures' genealogy-based chronology ends with the numbers of years and ages given for the patriarchs in

4

chapter 11 of Genesis. Importantly, the scriptures provide additional critical, nongenealogical evidence that enables us to accurately extend the biblical timeline to more than three thousand years after the creation and a thousand years after Abraham to King David and King Solomon.

In the next chapter, we will consider the chronology for the one-thousand-year period between Jacob and King Solomon.

CHAPTER 2

BIBLICAL CHRONOLOGY
FROM JACOB TO SOLOMON
AND THE FIRST TEMPLE

Isaac was sixty years old when he begat Esau and Jacob in 2108 AC (Genesis 25:26). Jacob entered Egypt with seventy family members (Genesis 46:27) when he was 130 years old, in the year 2238 AC (Genesis 47:9), and he died in Egypt seventeen years later at age 147 in 2255 AC (Genesis 47:28). Exodus 12:40–41 twice tells us that the time spent in Egypt by the Jews was 430 years.

Now the sojourning of the children of Israel, who dwelt in Egypt, was four hundred and thirty years … at the end of the four hundred and thirty years, even the selfsame day it came to pass, that all the hosts of the Lord went out from the land of Egypt.

This was the period of time from when Jacob and his family joined Joseph during the famine until Moses led the people out of bondage in Egypt. Numbers 33:3 tells us that Moses led the people out of Egypt on the fifteenth day of Nisan (the day after the Passover). Therefore, Jacob and his family entered Egypt on Nissan 15, 430 years earlier (Nissan 15, 2238 AC). The children of Israel were afflicted for four hundred of those years by the Egyptians, according to Genesis 15:13. The affliction would have begun thirty years after Jacob entered Egypt. Based on Jacob entering Egypt with his family in 2238 AC and the Exodus taking place 430 years later, the year of the Exodus was 2668 AC (2238 + 430).

The period of wandering, from the time Moses led the people out of Egypt in the Exodus until the death of Aaron, was forty years (Numbers 33:38). This makes the period of the Jews wandering in the wilderness from 2668 AC to 2708 AC (2668 + 40).

> And it came to pass in the four hundred and eightieth year after the children of Israel were come out of the land of Egypt, in the fourth year of Solomon's reign over Israel, in the month of Zif, which is the second month, that he began to build the house of the Lord. (1 Kings 6:1)

This critical scripture tells us that the building of the first temple began during the fourth year of Solomon's reign, 480 years after the Exodus. The Exodus was in 2668 AC, and so the building of the first temple began 480 years later in 3148 AC (2668 + 480 = 3148). With this scripture, a chronology and timeline extending from the creation to the period of King David and King Solomon and the first temple can be determined.

The scriptures are not specific, but they clearly imply that Solomon assumed the throne in the same year of David's death. Thus, construction of the temple began four years after David's death. David lived seventy years. Thus, he was born seventy-four years before construction of the first temple began. He assumed the throne when he was thirty years old, reigned for forty years, and died. Dating from the creation, David's chronology is as follows.

- David's birth (3148 - 74 = 3074) 3074 AC (2 Samuel 5:4)
- David became king (3148 - 44 = 3104) 3104 AC (2 Samuel 5:4)
- David's death (3148 - 4 = 3144) 3144 AC (1 Kings 2:11)

Solomon reigned for forty years. The year of his death marked the beginning of the divided kingdom, which is addressed in the next chapter.

- Solomon became king (upon the death of David) 3144 AC (1 Kings 2:11–12)
- Construction of the first temple began 3148 AC (1 Kings 6:1)
- Dedication of the first temple (seven years to build) 3155 AC (1 Kings 6:38)
- Death of Solomon 3184 AC (1 Kings 11:42)

Table 2 extends the postcreation chronology from Jacob to the death of Solomon. The period from Jacob's birth to Solomon's death was 1076 years (3184 - 2108 = 1076).

Table 2: Chronology from Jacob to Solomon

Event	Year	Scripture Reference
Birth of Jacob	2108 AC	Genesis 25:26
Start of Israelite sojourn in Egypt	2238 AC	Genesis 47:9
The Exodus	2668 AC	Exodus 12:40–41
End of 40 years in the wilderness	2708 AC	Numbers 14:34, 33:38
Birth of David	3074 AC	2 Samuel 5:4
Death of David; Solomon King	3144 AC	1 Kings 2:11–12
Construction of first temple	3148–3155 AC	1 Kings 6:1, 38
Dedication of first temple	3155 AC	1 Kings 6:38
Solomon's death	3184 AC	1 Kings 11:42

The 480th year in 1 Kings 6:1 is the critical link in Scripture that establishes the biblical chronology from the Exodus to the first temple. It also establishes the period of the judges from the death of Joshua to the time of King Saul to be about 350 years, although the chronological data given in the books of Joshua, Judges, and Samuel has been difficult to harmonize. What is important is that the Bible provides an unbroken chronology and timeline from the Creation through the patriarchs, to the 430 years in Egypt, to the Exodus and forty years in the wilderness, to the reign of Solomon and the construction and dedication of the first temple. Thus, the first 3,184 years of Bible history, from the Creation to Solomon's death, are established solely from Scripture.

From this point forward, an easily and continuously connected Old Testament, scripture-based chronology ends. Although significant chronological information is revealed for the period between the divided kingdom and the Babylonian captivity in the books of the Kings, it had been virtually impossible to resolve the apparent discrepancies and create a reliable chronology for this critical period until the midtwentieth century. In order to accurately extend our creation-based chronology and timeline forward—and to link it with the ancient historical chronology dating backwards from the modern era—we turn our attention to the work of Dr. Edwin R. Thiele in *The Mysterious Numbers of the Hebrew Kings* (1951) and his successful efforts to synchronize nearly five hundred years of critical Hebrew history with secular history. Dr Thiele's work provides the critical link between the post-creation chronology developed in the previous two chapters and the modern era.

CHAPTER 3

BIBLICAL CHRONOLOGY FOR THE PERIOD OF THE HEBREW KINGS AND THE ESTABLISHMENT OF AN ABSOLUTE DATE LINKING TWO HALVES OF BIBLE HISTORY

While the Bible provides a solid, scriptural chronology from the Creation to the time of King Solomon, the chronological information revealed in the Scriptures for the Hebrew kings during the period of the divided kingdom has long been a major stumbling block for Bible historians. In his book *The Mysterious Numbers of the Hebrew Kings*, master chronologist and theologian Dr. Edwin R. Thiele[1] brings much clarity and resolution to this ancient historical timeline by solving the mysterious and complex dates revealed in Scripture concerning the reigns of the kings of Judah, Israel, and their neighbors for the four-hundred-year period dating from Solomon's death and the divided kingdom to the post-Babylonian, Persian period. Most significant, he determined an "absolute" date for the beginning of the divided kingdom, thus enabling a complete chronological timeline that dates from the modern era back to the Creation.

What follows is a brief summary of Dr. Thiele's major findings to resolve problems that had long hindered the emergence of a reliable, harmonious chronology of the Hebrew kings, and that agrees with and supports the chronological data revealed in the books of Kings in the Bible. His major findings include the following.

1. Dr. Thiele's research reveals how the calendar was reckoned among the ancient kingdoms. He discovered that all the ancient kingdoms—Israel, Judah, Egypt, Assyria, Babylon, and Persia—used a lunar-solar calendar that measured time by lunar months and solar years. Since the moon makes a complete revolution around the earth in 29 1/2 days, the ancient calendar year consisted of twelve thirty-day months. But because this procedure gave a year that was approximately eleven days short of a solar year, it was necessary for frequent adjustments to be made. To resolve the annual eleven-day shortfall between lunar and solar calendar dating, each kingdom adjusted their calendar once every two or three years by adding a thirteenth month (intercalary month) to bring the lunar calendar back in alignment with the solar year. Seven intercalations were required every nineteen years to keep the lunar calendar aligned with the solar (365 day) year. Contemporary Hebrew calendars continue to function this way today. Appendix 2 shows the Hebrew calendar with the intercalary month of Adar 2 added seven times during the period from 2001–2021.

2. Dr. Thiele's research revealed that the northern kingdom of Israel and the southern kingdom of Judah reckoned their calendars and the reigns of their kings differently. All the ancient kingdoms began their calendar year in the spring, after the vernal equinox, with the month of Nisan as the first month on the Hebrew calendar. Thus, Israel and her neighbors reckoned their yearly calendars from Nisan to Nisan. But it was discovered that Judah was unique among all the ancient kingdoms in that Judah dated the reigns of

their kings from Tishri to Tishri, even though their "sacred" calendar was adjusted each year on the first day of Nisan to ensure a Passover date of 14–15 Nisan. Thus, in ancient times Judah had both a sacred (Nisan to Nisan) calendar and a civil (Tishri to Tishri) calendar—a fact that didn't become evident until the rebirth of Israel in 1948, when the Jews resumed Tishri to Tishri dating with a Hebrew civil calendar. Judah's Tishri to Tishri dating turns out to be a significant issue that caused problems for historians and chronologists, as will become clear in the next chapter when we deal with the issue of a "prophetic" year.

3. The second important difference between Israel and Judah was the way they reckoned the reigns of their kings. In the northern kingdom, Israel used the non-accession year system such that the year in which the king began to reign was the first year of his reign. This system resulted in double counting years because the year in which a king died was called his last year of reign, and the king assuming the throne called the same year his first year of reign. With this system of reckoning, there was always duplication of one year for each reign. In Judah, the accession year system was used such that the year in which a king died was his last year of reign, and the period remaining in that year until the first day of the next year (1 Tishri) was counted as the new king's accession year. This method eliminated the issue of double counting years.

With this understanding of how Israel and Judah reckoned their calendars (Nisan to Nisan and Tishri to Tishri dating, respectively) and the reigns of their kings (non-accession and accession year systems, respectively), Dr. Thiele was able to create a harmonious chronology for the kings of Israel and Judah that fully supports the data revealed in the first and second books of Kings.

His next task was to come up with an absolute date that fit the chronological timeline not only for the Hebrew kings but for the neighboring nations as well. From this absolute date, it would finally become possible to reckon both the Hebrew and non-Hebrew chronologies forward and backward from that date. Resolution of this issue is critical to linking the post-creation chronologies in chapters 1–2 of this book with the modern era. The research undertaken to determine an absolute date for the chronologies of Israel, Judah, and their neighbors is detailed in chapter 4 of Dr. Thiele's book. What follows are highlights from his efforts to determine an absolute date from which all the chronologies could be harmonized.

Because all the ancient kingdoms reckoned their calendars the same way, it was difficult if not impossible for chronologists to link specific events in one kingdom with those in another kingdom on the same timeline, unless the same significant event appeared in the chronologies of at least two separate ancient calendars. Dr. Thiele identified Assyria as having a unique procedure in reckoning their annual calendars among all the ancient kingdoms. He makes the following statement about Assyria's unique calendar system.

> Assyria possessed a system of eponymous years that served a similar purpose to that of the eras used by other nations, except that the eponym was for a period of just one year ... Assyria followed the practice each year of appointing to the office of eponym, or limmu, some high official of the court. The limmu held office for a calendar year and to that year was given the name of the individual then occupying the position of limmu. Historical events in Assyria were normally dated in terms of these limmus. Fortunately, the Assyrians followed the custom of preserving the lists of eponyms (each named for a specific limmu), many of which are available today.[2]

Dr. Thiele then identified two specific points of contact between Assyria and Israel that ultimately led to the determination of his absolute date. The Assyrian chronologies reveal that Ahab, king of Israel, was allied against Assyrian King Shalamanezer III at the battle of Qarqar in the sixth year of Shalmanezer's reign, and that Jehu, king of Israel, paid tribute to Shalamanezer in the eighteenth year of his reign. Based on the names assigned as limmus for the Assyrian calendar years in which these events took place, Dr. Thiele was able to determine that the battle of Qarqar took place in 853 BC (the battle in which Ahab died; 1 Kings 22:34–38) and that Jehu paid tribute to Shalmanezer in 841 BC (the first year of Jehu's reign). These links led to the synchronization of Israel's and her neighbors' chronologies for the entire period of the Hebrew kings.

With 853 fixed as the last year of Ahab, Dr. Thiele was able to accurately determine that the period of time from Ahab's death backward to the year of Jeroboam's accession to the throne of Israel and the division of the kingdom was seventy-eight years and seven days. This secured the date for the divided kingdom of 931–930 BC.

Dr. Thiele said this about the absolute date: "Having fixed 931/930 as the year of the division of the monarchy and the beginning of the nations of Israel and Judah, I will proceed forward with the chronological pattern for the Hebrew rulers based on the Masoretic Text. In the interests of simplicity the date 930 is being used for the division of the kingdom instead of 931/930."[3]

Dr. Thiele's selection of the year 930 over 931 as the absolute year is based on the way the two kingdoms reckoned years. For Israel's scribes, the year 931 ran from Nisan 931 to Nisan 930 (9 months in 931 and 3 months in 930), whereas Judah's scribes recorded 931 from Tishri 931 to Tishri 930 (3 months in 931 and 9 months in 930). Because much of the Masoretic Text was written by Judean scribes who reckoned years from Tishri, 930 became the absolute year of record.

The result of Dr. Thiele's efforts is displayed at the beginning of his book in the table labeled "The Data and Dates of the Rulers of Judah and Israel in Their Order of Sequence." Highlights from the table are shown in Table 3 below.

Table 3: Highlights of Chronological Data for the Rulers of Judah and Israel[4]

Name/Event	Nation	Period/Date
Rehoboam	Judah	930–913 BC
Jeroboam 1	Israel	930–909 BC
Ahab	Israel	874–853 BC
Jehu	Israel	841–814 BC
Hoshea- last king of Israel	Israel	732–723 BC
Israel falls to the the Assyrians	Israel	723 BC
Josiah	Judah	640–609 BC
Nebucudnezzar's 1st siege of Jerusalem. Start of 70 year captivity	Judah	605 BC
Jehoahaz	Judah	(3 mos) 609 BC
Jehoiachin	Judah	598–597 BC
Zedekiah- last king of Judah	Judah	597–586 BC

In concluding his work, Dr. Thiele extended the chronology forward from the end of the Babylonian captivity to include the chronology for the Persian kings, which links other important dates and events in Scripture. He noted that "The canon of Ptolemy is completely reliable. It did not pretend to give a complete list of all the rulers of either Babylon or Persia... but it was a device that made possible the correct allocation into a broad chronological scheme."[5] The rulers of Persia, according to the Canon of Ptolemy and endorsed by Thiele, are shown in Table 4 below.

Table 4: Chronology of the Rulers of Persia According to Ptolemy[6]

Ruler	Length of Reign	Years of the Christian Era
Cyrus	9	538–530 BC
Cambysus	8	529–522 BC
Darius I	36	521–486 BC

Xerxes (Ahasuerus)	21	485–465 BC
Artaxerxes I	41	464–424 BC
Darius II	19	423–405 BC
Artaxerxes II	46	404–359 BC
Ochus	21	358–338 BC
Arses	2	337–336 BC
Darius III	4	335–332 BC
Total years	**206 years***	

* The following is noted from Appendix G, "The Seder Olam Rabbah—Why Jewish Dating Is Different," in James Ussher's *Annals of the World*. The authors note that in defining the period of the second temple, Jewish Rabbi Yose Ben Halafta (died AD 160), who compiled the Seder Olam or Book of the Order of the World, which is the basis for the modern Hebrew calendar, reckoned the second temple period from 351 BC to 70 AD, whereas virtually all non-Jewish chronologists reckoned the period from 515 BC to 70 AD. This is a difference of 164 years, all of which was taken from the Persian period, and it makes the period of the Persian kings only 53 years in length as opposed to the 206 years chronicled above. The authors of Appendix G state,

> The result of this shortening of the span of the Persian Empire is that the paramount prophecy and major foundation block of chronology—the Daniel 9:25 seventy weeks of years—has become dislodged. Furthermore, this shortening as perpetuated within the Seder Olam was deliberate... it is manifestly apparent that the real reasons for the deliberate altering of their own national chronology in the Seder Olam were (1) to conceal the fact that the Daniel 9:25 prophecy clearly pointed to Jesus of Nazareth as its fulfillment, and (2) to make the seventy weeks of years prophecy point instead to Simon Bar Kokhba in 135 AD as the Messiah.[7]

This is one of the most significant reasons why the Hebrew calendar remains out of sync with Christian era chronology, even today.

From Dr. Thiele's work to establish an absolute date for the divided kingdom, an accurate chronology for the Hebrew kings and from Ptolemy's chronology for the Persian kings, nearly 600 additional years can be reckoned with the 3,184 years dating from creation to Solomon—all from Scripture. Importantly, it is now possible to reconcile the AC dates with the BC dates and link the two halves of Old Testament Bible history together. Because we know that Solomon died in 3184 AC, or 3,184 years after the Creation, and the absolute date determined by Dr. Thiele for Solomon's death and the divided kingdom is established as 930 BC, the Creation was in 4114 BC (3184 + 930). It is interesting that the creation date of 4114 BC differs by only 110 years from the 4004 BC date determined by Ussher in 1659.[8] Table 5 shows the resultant AC and BC date conversions for the major personages and events dating from the Creation to the decree of Artaxerxes, which directed the rebuilding of Jerusalem as defined in Daniel 9:25.

Table 5: Bible Chronology from the Creation to the Decree of Artaxerxes

Person/Event	AC date(s)	BC date(s)	Date/Verse/Note
The Creation	0	4114 BC	Genesis chapter 1
Birth of Noah	1056 AC	3058 BC	
The Genesis Flood	1656 AC	2458 BC	
Death of Noah	2006 AC	2108 BC	
Life of Abraham	1948–2123 AC	2166–1991 BC	Note (1) below
Birth of Jacob	2108 AC	2006 BC	
Start of Israel's sojourn in Egypt	2238 AC	1876 BC	15 Nisan (April 7, 1876 BC)
The Exodus	2668 AC	1446 BC	April 24, 1446 BC/ Note (2)
Aaron's death; end 40 years in wilderness	2708 AC	1406 BC	Numbers 20:28, 33:38–39
Birth of David	3074 AC	1040 BC	
Death of David; Solomon king	3144 AC	970 BC	
Seven yr construction of the first temple	3148–3155 AC	966–959 BC	

Dedication of the first Temple	3155 AC	959 BC	1 Kings 6:38
Solomon's death; divided kingdom	3184 AC	930 BC	First **Absolute date**
Hoshea, last king of Israel	3382–3391 AC	732–723 BC	
Destruction of Israel by the Assyrians	3391 AC	723 BC	
Josiah reign	3474–3505 AC	640–609 BC	
Jehoiakim reign	3505–3516 AC	609–598 BC	
Nebucudnezzar's siege; 70-year captivity	3509 AC	605 BC	Note (3)
Jerusalem besieged; king taken captive	3517 AC	597 BC	March 16, 597 BC/ Note (4)
Jerusalem fell; temple destroyed	3528 AC	586 BC	July 18, 586 BC/ Note (5)
Decree by Cyrus ending captivity	3582–3581 AC	538–537 BC	2 Ch 36:22–23; Ezra 1:1–3
Period of 70-year Babylonian captivity	3509–3579 AC	605– **535** BC	Ezra 3:1–2,8/ Note (6)
Period of 70-year Temple desolation	3528-3599 AC	586-515 BC	Note (6)
Completion of 2nd temple under Darius I	3599 AC	515 BC	Ezra 6:15
Esther rises to queen of Persia	3628 AC	478 BC	Esther 2:16
Artaxerxes decree to rebuild Jerusalem	3670 AC	444 BC	Dan 9:25; Neh 2:1/ Note (7)

Notes

1. Some scholars, including Ussher, interpreted Genesis 11:26–27, 32 and Genesis 12:4 to mean that Abraham was Terah's youngest son, born when he was 130 years old and not 70, as indicated above and in Table 1. Dr. Morris comments on this in his study Bible:

   > According to Genesis 12:4, Abram left Haran for Canaan when he was 75 years old, which would have been 130 years before Terah's death, if indeed Abram had been born when Terah was 70 years old (11:26). Yet Stephen, in Acts 7:8 says that Abram did not leave

Haran until his father was dead. Probably Stephen was suggesting that Terah, though still alive physically, had "died" as far as God's will and calling to him were concerned, using the terminology that Christ had used in advising a young man in a similar situation (Ma 8:21–22). Otherwise, Abram would have been born when Terah was 130 years old—*a very unlikely circumstance in view of the special miracle required for Abram himself to have a son when he was only 100.*[9] (emphasis added)

Fortunately, by dating Abraham from the creation in Table 1, if it could be confirmed that Abram was born when Terah was 130, the change would merely push the dates from before Abraham back to the creation date by 60 years (making the creation date 4174), but it would not affect the BC timeline or chronology and dating after Abraham's death.

2. The exact dates for Israel's entrance to and exit from Egypt, based on Exodus 12:41 and Numbers 33:3, were computed with 15 Nisan marking the day after first full moon following the vernal equinox of that year and do not consider the intercalary month dating that the Jews may have used to determine the dates (unlikely at the time). More information on the Exodus Passover date is presented in Appendix 2.

3. Nebuchadnezzar came against Jerusalem in the third year of Jehoiakim (Daniel 1:1), which was also the twenty-third year of Jeremiah's warnings (Jeremiah 25:1, 3). Daniel and his companions were taken captive, and the Babylonian captivity began (summer of 605 BC).

4. In Nebuchadnezzar's eighth year, he besieged Jerusalem and took Jehoiachin captive to Babylon. The prophet Ezekiel was among the exiles taken to Babylon in 597 BC.

5. Ezekiel received word from the Lord (Ezekiel 24:1–2, 6) on the very day the final siege of Jerusalem began: on the tenth day of the tenth month of the ninth year (January 15, 588 BC), when Nebuchadnezzar marched against Jerusalem with his whole army. Jerusalem fell on the ninth day of the fourth month of the eleventh year of Zedekiah, the nineteenth year of Nebuchadnezzar (2 Kings 25:2–3, 8), which was July 18, 586 BC.

6. Dr. Morris comments on Ezra 3:8 in a note on Ezra 3:1 in the Morris Study Bible:

> This gathering in Jerusalem and reinstitution of the sacrifices *(3:2)* (7th month of the 3rd year after Cyrus conquered Babylon) probably marks the end of the 70 year exile predicted by Jeremiah (Je 25:11–12; Dan 9:2). Although exact dates are uncertain, many authorities (including Dr. Thiele) believe that the exile began in 605 BC and the return to begin rebuilding the temple was in about 535 BC [70 years].[10]

The total period from the laying of the second temple foundation to its completion (sixth year of Darius; Nehemiah 6:15) was about twenty years (535–515 BC). There are some who interpret the seventy-year period described in Jeremiah 29:10 as the period from the destruction of the first temple in 586 to the completion of the second temple in 515. In either case, seventy years is fulfilled for both the time of the captivity of the people and the period of time between the two temples. The dates in Table 5 support both views.

7. Artaxerxes was king of Persia from 464–424 BC. Nehemiah 2:1 indicates that it was the month of Nisan in the twentieth year of Artaxerxes' reign when Nehemiah was given the letter (decree) from the king to rebuild Jerusalem. Artaxerxes'

twentieth year was 445–444 BC. Dr. Thiele says this about the date:

> It is clear from Nehemiah 1:1 and 2:1 that Nehemiah reckoned the years of the Persian king Artaxerxes from Tishri to Tishri, for the month of Kislev (Nov/Dec) fell within the twentieth year of the king and the following Nisan was still in the same twentieth year. But why would Nehemiah do this, when the custom in Persia was to reckon the year from Nisan to Nisan? Is it not possible to suppose that Nehemiah was acquainted with the custom formerly followed by the kings of Judah to begin their regnal years with Tishri and, in the spirit of intense nationalism, applied the customary Jewish practice to a Persian king. In the double-dated Aramaic papyri from Elephantine of the fifth century B.C., the reigns of Persian kings were also dated according to Judean Tishri years rather than Persian Nisan years.[11]

This means that the month of Nisan in the 20th year of Artaxerxes was in 444 BC, and not 445 BC as Sir Robert Anderson (next chapter) and others have claimed.

Now, both halves of Bible history are linked to the absolute date of 930 BC for the divided kingdom and result in a harmonious, reliable chronology dating from the Creation forward 3,670 years to the decree of Artaxerxes in 444 BC and backward from the absolute date of 930 BC to the creation in 4114 BC.

Next, we will consider the chronology for the period from Artaxerxes to the incarnate Jesus Christ.

CHAPTER 4

THE PERIOD BETWEEN THE DECREE OF ARTAXERXES AND THE INCARNATE JESUS CHRIST

Daniel's Seventy-Week Prophecy and The Coming Prince

In researching the period from the decree of Artaxerxes to the first advent of Jesus Christ, I was fully aware this would be a difficult and likely controversial portion of the chronology to resolve. Prior to my work on the Christmas star and recent discoveries in *The Mysterious Numbers of the Hebrew Kings*, like many Christians, I believed in the correctness of the work done by Sir Robert Anderson in *The Coming Prince* (1894) and his now famous and generally accepted prophecy for the first sixty-nine weeks defined in Daniel 9:25 that, he claimed, links the decree of the Persian king Artaxerxes to rebuild Jerusalem to the first advent of Jesus Christ.

Believing that Anderson had resolved the date for the Palm Sunday before Jesus's crucifixion as April 6, 32 AD, I was surprised when my 2013 Christmas star research pointed to a crucifixion date for Jesus of April 3, 33 AD. Thus, my date for the public advent of Messiah the Prince was Palm Sunday, March 29, 33 AD, one year after Anderson's date of April 6, 32 AD. The chronological resource used for the Christmas star research was Ussher's *Annals of the World* (1659), which predated Anderson by more than two hundred years. Although both Ussher and Anderson conclude in their respective works that the birth of Jesus had to take place by the year 4 BC (primarily based on the writings of Josephus regarding the date for the death of Herod), Ussher proposed the April 3, 33 AD date for Christ's crucifixion, which agrees with the Christmas star date. Fully aware of this discrepancy with Anderson's date, I obtained a copy of *The Coming Prince* (tenth edition, 1957) to research for this book.

Analysis of Sir Robert Anderson's "Prophetic" Year

The culminating statement in Sir Robert Anderson's book on the sixty-nine-week prophecy in Daniel 9:25 is,

> What was the length of the period intervening between the issuing of the decree to rebuild Jerusalem and the public advent of "Messiah the Prince"—between the 14th of March, B.C. 445 and the 6th of April, A.D. 32? The interval contained exactly and to the very day 173,880 days, or seven times sixty-nine prophetic years of 360 days, the first sixty-nine weeks of Gabriel's prophecy.[1]

The claim made Anderson famous. In his book, he also made the following additional claims based on his defined "prophetic" year (twelve thirty-day months equate to a "prophetic" 360-day year).

1. "Now from the tenth day of Tebeth B.C. 589 to the twenty-fourth day of Chisleu B.C. 520, was a period of 25,202 days. We may conclude, therefore, that the era of desolations (70 year captivity) was a period of seventy years of 360 days,

beginning the day after the Babylonian army invested Jerusalem, and ending on the day before the foundation of the second temple was laid."[2]

2. "From the year succeeding the dedication of Solomon's temple, to the year before the foundation of the second temple was laid, was a period of 490 years of 360 days."[3]

3. "Now the seventieth week is admittedly a period of seven years, and half of this period is three times described as "a time, times and half a time," or "the dividing of a time"; twice as forty-two months and twice as 1,260 days. But 1,260 days is exactly equal to forty-two months of thirty days, or three and a half years of 360 days, whereas three and a half Julian years contain 1,278 days. It follows therefore that the prophetic year is not the Julian year, but the ancient year of 360 days."[4]

Anderson concludes that the seven-year Tribulation will be exactly 2,520 days in length. This equates to 6 years and 327 days in solar years. Each claim will be addressed separately and compared with the chronology developed in chapter 3, but first we will consider the issue of a prophetic year. Sir Robert Anderson appears to be the first to define a prophetic year and to apply a calendar of 360-day years (twelve thirty-day months) to the ancient chronologies, even though others like Isaac Newton in the 1600s and Julius Africanus in his chronology of the seventy weeks in about AD 240 refer to a year as being 360 days based on twelve thirty-day months. In an online article on the subject, Grant Jeffery indicates that Newton, Africanus and others referenced one or more examples in the Bible as they pointed to a 360-day year: (1) Abraham, the father of Israel, continued to use the 360-day year, which was known in his home in Ur of the Chaldees. (2) The Genesis account of the flood in the days of Noah illustrated this 360-day year by recording the 150-day interval (five thirty-day months) till the waters abated from the earth. The 150 days began on the seventeenth day of the second month and ended on the seventeenth day of the seventh month (Genesis 7:11,

24; Genesis 8:3–4). (3) The book of Esther (1:4) indicates the same 360-day length of year by recording the six-month-long feast of Xerxes (Ahaseurus) continuing exactly 180 days. (4) The Prophet Daniel recorded that the time of the absolute power of the antichrist over the nations will last three and one-half years (Daniel 7:25). John, in the book of Revelation, described this same three-and-one-half-year period (Revelation 13:5–7) as consisting of forty-two months of thirty days each, totaling 1,260 days (Revelation 11:2–3; Revelation 12:6).[5]

Even though biblical writers describe the ancient 360-day year and fractions thereof in both the historical and prophetic parts of Scripture, there is no chronological evidence in the ancient records that specifically identifies a functioning 360-day annual calendar. Neither is any reference made prior to Anderson of multiple years or an extended period of time (like the seventy-year captivity) being defined in terms of literal 360-day or "prophetic" years and used on any ancient calendar.

In *The Coming Prince*, Anderson makes the following statements to support his case for the prophetic year.

(1.) "That the Jewish year was lunisolar appears to be reasonably certain."[6] This is a true statement. A lunisolar calendar was an annual calendar defined by the lunar cycle that required frequent adjustment to coincide with a solar year in order to account for the seasons. What was not clearly understood until the midtwentieth century is that *all* the ancient nations (or at least Israel and her neighbors) used a lunisolar calendar based on twelve thirty-day months. As Dr. Thiele pointed out in chapter 3,

> frequent adjustments had to be made to keep the year in line with the sun and annual seasons. Such adjustments were made whenever necessary by the addition of an intercalary month to the yearly calendar. Thus once every two or three years- seven intercalations within a nineteen year period- the

calendar contained thirteen months instead of twelve.[7]

Also, all the nations, including Judah, made their calendar adjustment in the spring with the vernal equinox so that the month of Nisan began the yearly cycle.

(2.) In discussing the Nativity, Anderson made the following statement regarding one of his key historical resources, apparently without amplifying evidence: "And, therefore, since Josephus always reckons his years from Nisan to Nisan, and counts the initial and terminal fractions of Nisan as complete years..."[8] Although Exodus 12:2 clearly reveals that Moses was told by God to make Nisan the first month (it continues to be the first month on the Jewish sacred calendar), Dr. Thiele's discovery that Judah alone among the ancients reckoned regnal years from Tishri to Tishri, at least throughout the period of the Hebrew kings, later caused significant and irreconcilable problems for chronologists who attempted to reckon Judean years from Nisan to Nisan. He further determined that among the prophetic writings of Judah, including those during the Babylonian captivity, Tishri years were used in the books of Kings and Daniel, and Nisan years were used in Babylonian records and in the books of Jeremiah and Ezekiel. After the captivity, Dr. Thiele believed Ezra and Nehemiah reverted back to Tishri years because the chronologies for both Israel and its neighbors remained harmonious by doing so. Therefore because Josephus was a Judean Jew writing in the first century, it may very well be that his reckoning was Tishri to Tishri and not Nisan to Nisan, as Anderson insists.

Because all the ancient nations reckoned a 360-day year of twelve thirty-day months, it makes complete sense that fractions of a year would be referenced in like manner: half a year being 180 days, and a quarter of year being 90 days. This is precisely what the Scriptures do. It must be remembered that the number 360 is a convenient compromise that does not align with either a lunar year (12 × 29.5 = 354 days) or a solar year (365 1/4 days). A 360-day year is six days longer than a lunar calendar year and 5 1/4 days shorter than a solar calendar year. Regardless of how each ancient kingdom reckoned their lunisolar calendar, they all made adjustments that accounted for the four seasons (spring, summer, fall, and winter) based on the vernal and autumnal equinoxes and summer and winter solstices that define each solar year. Importantly, regardless of the overage or shortfall in the number of days when adjustments were made in ancient calendars to align with the solar year, there was never any carryover added to or subtracted from a succeeding year, and such changes never accumulated over an extended number of solar years.

Carryovers, shortages, and the alignment of each year with the seasons pose significant problems for Anderson's prophetic year, and they are issues he never addressed. In Exodus 12:2, God told Moses that the month of the Passover, Nisan (March/April), would be "the first month of the year to you." This made spring the first season of the year. In Leviticus 23, God established the Sabbath (23:3) and the feasts of the Lord as holy convocations that the people were required to "proclaim in their seasons." The first four feasts, Passover (23:4–5), Unleavened Bread (23:6–8), First Fruits (23:9–14), and Pentecost (23:15–22), were the spring feasts, and Trumpets (23:23–24), Day of Atonement (23:26–32) and Tabernacles (23:33–42) were the fall feasts. Included in God's declarations for the feasts was an accompanying admonition that each feast "shall be a statute forever throughout your generations in all your dwellings." Thus, the seven feasts were to be celebrated by the Jews *annually* (every solar year) in the spring and fall. Additionally, in Leviticus 25, God proclaims the law of the Sabbath year, or *Shemitah*, to be observed every seventh year, and the Jubilee year, which was to be hallowed every fiftieth year. Again, these Sabbaths were to be observed as required based on the solar year, not a lunar or prophetic year.

For short periods of time like the seven years that define a week of years, the Shemitah, or the seventieth week, the difference between Anderson's 360-day prophetic year and a 365 1/4–day solar year is 5 1/4 days per year, or 36 3/4 days in seven years. Chronologically, this difference of about one month's time may not be significant when rounding to the nearest year because the period would be defined as seven years in either case. But when the period defined by a prophetic year (360-day year) is seventy years or longer, significant problems begin to arise. Seventy years of 360 days is 25,200 days, whereas for 365 1/4–day solar years, the period is 25,567 3/4 days—a difference of 367 3/4 days or a period of more than a solar year. Now, an entire year is unaccounted for in Anderson's prophetic year reckoning. The problem only gets worse with longer periods of time like 490 years. Reckoning 490 prophetic years of 360 days equates to 176,400 days, but 490 solar years is 178,973 days. These 2,573 days result in a difference of 7.04 solar years that contain 28 seasons, one Shemitah, and 49 feasts of the Lord that are never accounted for and would essentially disappear from history based on Anderson's prophetic year calendar. It is difficult to imagine how chronologists could ever resolve historical dates based on prophetic year reckoning.

Analysis of Anderson's Claims Based on a "Prophetic" Year

In view of these facts, let us now evaluate the three claims made by Sir Anderson at the beginning of this chapter before considering his interpretation of Daniel's sixty-nine-week prophecy in Daniel 9:25. Each claim will be compared with the Bible chronology in Chapter 3, Table 5.

1. Now from the tenth day of Tebeth B.C. 589 to the twenty-fourth day of Chisleu B.C. 520, was a period of 25,202 days. We may conclude, therefore, that the era of desolations (70 year captivity) was a period of seventy years of 360 days, beginning the day after the Babylonian army invested Jerusalem, and ending on the day before the foundation of the second temple was laid.[9]

Anderson's claim is that the period of the Babylonian captivity was from 589–520 BC, a period of 70 prophetic years or 69.04 solar years. Notes 4 and 5 in Table 5 indicate that Nebuchadnezzar began his third and final siege of Jerusalem in his seventeenth year (January 15, 588 BC) and captured the city in his nineteenth year on July 18, 586 BC. Importantly, this is nineteen years after Nebuchadnezzar's first siege of Jerusalem in 605 BC. In fact, 605 BC is the year that scholars, including Drs. Thiele and Morris, believe marked the beginning of the Babylonian captivity (Table 5). Anderson's claim that the captivity ended in 520 BC, the day before the foundation for the second temple was laid, has no scriptural basis. Scholars agree that the captivity officially ended in about 535 BC when the remnant of Jews who returned to Jerusalem began to lay the foundation for the second temple (Table 5, note 6). The scriptures provide no specific dating information about when the foundation for the second temple was laid, but Ezra 3:1–2 seems to confirm that this happened within two years of Cyrus's decree in 538–37 BC, making the year of the laying of the second temple foundation about 535 BC. The temple was completed in 515 BC during the sixth year of Darius (Table 4). Upon comparing Anderson's claim with the Table 5 chronology for the period of the seventy-year Babylonian captivity, we get the following.

Event	Anderson	(Table 5)	Difference
Beginning of Babylonian captivity	589 BC	605BC	16 years
Laying of 2nd temple foundation	520 BC	535 BC	15 years
Length of captivity (solar years)	69 years	70 years	

I believe Anderson's claim is incorrect. His chronology is off by fifteen to sixteen years, and by his reckoning, the period of captivity was only sixty-nine solar years, not seventy years as defined in Scripture.

2. From the year succeeding the dedication of Solomon's temple, to the year before the foundation of the second temple was laid, was a period of 490 years of 360 days.[10]

In his second claim, Anderson states that the period from the year after the dedication of Solomon's temple to the year before the second temple foundation was laid was 490 prophetic years of 360

29

days. This equates to 483 solar years. Anderson claimed the second temple foundation was laid in 520 BC. By comparing Anderson's claim with the Table 5 chronology, we get:

Event	Anderson	(table 5)	Difference
Year after 1st temple dedication	1004 BC	958 BC	46 years
Year before 2nd temple foundation	521 BC	536 BC	15 years
Length of period (solar years)	483 years	422 years	

There is no reference in the Bible to the period from the year after the dedication of the first temple to the year before the laying of the second temple foundation as being a period of 490 years. Therefore, adding 490 prophetic years (483 solar years) to Anderson's 521 BC date gives a first temple dedication date of 1004 BC. From the chronology in Table 5, we see that Solomon dedicated the first temple in 959 BC (the eleventh year of his reign), and the foundation for the second temple was laid in about 535 BC. These events span a period of just 422 years, not the 490 prophetic years claimed by Anderson. Thus, Anderson's claim is incorrect, mainly due to problems with his chronology and the unfounded assertion that the period between the two events was 490 years, prophetic or otherwise.

3. Now the seventieth week is admittedly a period of seven years, and half of this period is three times described as "a time, times and half a time," or "the dividing of a time"; twice as forty two months and twice as 1,260 days. But 1,260 days is exactly equal to forty-two months of thirty days, or three and a half years of 360 days, whereas three and a half Julian years contain 1,278 days. It follows therefore that the prophetic year is not the Julian year, but the ancient year of 360 days.[11]

As previously discussed, the difference between seven prophetic years and seven solar years is a little more than one month (thirty-seven days). Here, Anderson asserts that Daniel's seventieth week will be a period of exactly 2,520 days, or about six solar years and eleven months. This prophecy has not yet come to pass, and it is unclear why Anderson would make this claim about an exact day or number of days for an event that Christians will not be present to witness. The Church (body of Christ) will not be on the earth when this event (the Tribulation) happens, and it is highly unlikely that anyone living through this most horrific seven-year period will be marking their calendars to confirm the exact number of days for the duration of the tribulation. It will undoubtedly seem like an eternity. Revelation 11:3 tells us that God's two witnesses will have power and prophesy for a thousand two hundred and three score (1,260) days. Most scholars believe the witnesses are killed at the midpoint of the tribulation, thus making it quite possible that the tribulation will be exactly 2,520 or 2 x 1,260 days. But, this number, as revealed in scripture, has nothing to do with Anderson's prophetic year reckoning.

Finally, let's consider Anderson's primary claim involving the sixty-nine-week period prophesied in Daniel 9:25.

> Know therefore and understand, that from the going forth of the commandment to restore and build Jerusalem unto the Messiah the Prince shall be seven weeks and threescore and two weeks: the street shall be built again, and the wall, even in troublesome times. (Daniel 9:25)

The seven weeks and three score and two weeks, or sixty-nine weeks, equates to 483 solar years. This is an important passage because it is the only verse in Scripture that chronologically attempts to link the period of time between the return of the Jews from the captivity with the first coming of Jesus Christ. What follows is Anderson's claim:

> What was the length of the period intervening between the issuing of the decree to rebuild Jerusalem and the public advent of "Messiah the Prince"—between the 14th of March, B.C. 445 and

31

the 6th of April, A.D. 32? The interval contained exactly and to the very day 173,880 days or seven times sixty nine prophetic years of 360 days, the first sixty-nine weeks of Gabriel's prophecy.[12]

This claim contains multiple issues and concerns, aside from those previously expressed concerning a prophetic year.

1. Anderson's starting point is the year 445 BC based on the reign of Artaxerxes (464–424 BC), defined in Table 5. Artaxerxes' twentieth year (Nehemiah 2:1) was 445–444 BC. From note 7 in Table 5, Dr. Thiele indicates that Nehemiah reckoned years from Tishri to Tishri, which means that the king's twentieth year was from Tishri 445 to Tishri 444 BC. The month of Nisan in that Tishri year was in 444, not 445 as Anderson determined from Nisan to Nisan reckoning. Thus, from the outset of his calculations, Anderson's chronology was off by one year.

2. March 14, 445 BC, was the first of Nisan according to Anderson (my Starry Night astronomy software shows the new moon over Jerusalem on March 13 and the Passover moon on March 27, 445 BC). Nevertheless, Nehemiah 2:1 does not mention the day of the month when the decree was issued: "And it came to pass *in the month of Nisan* in the twentieth year of Artaxerxes the king…" (Nehemiah 2:1). Thus, Anderson's starting point for his 173,880-day calculation is 1 Nisan as opposed to the actual day of the month, which is not recorded in Scripture.

3. Most, if not all, prophecy experts interpret the event described in Daniel 9:25 (the advent of "Messiah the Prince") to be Christ's triumphal entry to Jerusalem on Palm Sunday, five days before his crucifixion (Zechariah 9:9; Luke 19:37–38). Anderson believed the Triumphal entry and thus Palm Sunday was on April 6, 32 AD based on his prophetic year calculation. But, the date for the Passover in

AD 32 was April 14, eight days after Anderson's Triumphal entry date, not five days in accordance with Scripture. An additional complication is that the April 14, 32 AD Passover was on a Monday, not a Friday as the Scriptures seem to indicate (John 12:1, 12). Jesus came to Bethany "six days before the Passover" (John 12:1), and "On the next day" he entered Jerusalem in his Triumphal entry. The dates and days of the week for the Passovers between AD 25 and 37 are shown below.

Passover Dates from AD 25–37[13]

AD	Day	Date	AD	Day	Date
25	Sunday	April 1	32	Monday	April 14
26	Thursday	March 21	**33**	**Friday**	**April 3**
27	Wednesday	April 9	34	Tuesday	March 23
28	Monday	March 29	35	Monday	April 11
29	Sunday	April 17	36	Friday	March 30
30	Thursday	April 6	37	Thursday	April 18
31	Tuesday	March 27			

Anderson was aware of these Passover dates (chapter 8 in his book), and he devoted a chapter, "The Paschal Supper" (chapter 9) to explaining and justifying how the Passover on a Monday, with a Triumphal entry two Sundays (eight days) earlier, fits with Scripture. As the table shows, AD 33 and AD 36 are the only Passovers during the twelve-year period that fall on a Friday. Thus, Anderson's solution for the first 69 weeks of Daniel's 70 week prophecy—that there were 173,880 days (483 years × 360 days) between 1 Nisan/ March 14, 445 BC and Palm Sunday on April 6, 32 AD (eight days before the April 14 Passover)—does not fit with Scripture. He made this claim despite the facts that Artaxerxes' decree was issued sometime *during* the month of Nisan, not on 1 Nisan in 445 BC, and that his date for Palm Sunday (April 6, 32 AD) was two Sundays (eight days) before the Monday Passover on April 14, 32 AD.

Conclusions Regarding Anderson's Prophetic Year and Daniel's Sixty-Nine-Week Prophecy

Because Anderson miscalculated his dates by one year when reckoning from Nisan to Nisan, I attempted to calculate the date for Artaxerxes' decree, working backward from Palm Sunday, March 29, 33 AD (five days before Christ's crucifixion on the April 3, 33 AD Passover) using Anderson's prophetic 173,880-day (483 years of 360 days) standard. I assumed the simple solution would be to determine the difference in the number of days between the AD 32 and AD 33 dates and then add that same number days to the 1 Nisan 445 BC date in order to maintain the 173,880-day constant and move the calendar forward by one prophetic year. The simple math is that the difference between April 6, 32 AD and March 29, 33 AD is 357 days. If we add those 357 days to Anderson's March 14, 445 BC (1 Nisan) date, the 173,880-day constant would be maintained, and it resolves the problem, right? Wrong! This is because there is no such thing as a 360-day prophetic year in the real world. By adding 357 days to March 14, 445 BC, we get a date of March 6, 444 BC. But in 444 BC, 1 Nisan was on April 1, not March 6. March 6, 444 BC, was twenty-four days before the month of Nisan began, in the twelfth month of Adar.

Nehemiah 2:1 is clear that Artaxerxes' decree was issued in the month of Nisan, so what is the problem? The problem is this: The period from 1 Nisan 445 (March 14) to 1 Nisan 444 (April 1) is 383 days, whereas the period from the April 14, 32 AD, Passover to the April 3, 33 AD, Passover is only 357 days, a difference of 26 days. This means that an intercalary month (Adar 2) must have been added by the ancients, probably in 444, to bring the lunar calendar back in line with the solar year. This is exactly what had to be done (seven times every nineteen years) to adjust for the difference in lunar-solar dating. Unfortunately, no such mechanism exists with Anderson's prophetic year calendar calculations. The way lunar-solar reckoning is done with the Hebrew calendar today simply appears to coincide with the way it was done by the ancients (see Appendix 2).

So what is the answer to the sixty-nine-week prophecy of Daniel 9:25? I believe the sixty-nine weeks of years in the prophecy contains 483 solar years of 365 1/4 days and not 483 prophetic years of 360 days, or "exactly 173,880 days." Nevertheless, this does not solve the problem if it is true that Artaxerxes' decree was issued in 444 BC and the advent of "Messiah the Prince" was Palm Sunday in AD 33. This is a difference of 477 solar years, not the 483 years required by Scripture. If we count backward 483 years from AD 33, we get the year 450 BC, a date six years before Artaxerxes' decree was issued to Nehemiah. Ussher's date for Artaxerxes' decree is 454 BC, ten years before the 444 BC date. The Scriptures reveal two decrees that were issued during the reign of Artaxerxes. Ezra 7:8, 11, 13 tells us that Artaxerxes issued a decree to Ezra in the fifth month of the seventh year of his reign in 457 BC. This was followed thirteen years later with the letter given to Nehemiah (Nehemiah 2:8) issued in the month of Nisan during the twentieth year of Artaxerxes' reign in 445–444 BC. Although it is clear that the decree issued to Ezra was for provisions for worship in the temple, it leaves open the possibility that one or more additional decrees or letters may have been issued during the thirteen-year period between 457 and 444 BC but not recorded in Scripture, although this seems unlikely. The other possibility is that the chronology is wrong and that Artaxerxes' twentieth year may not have been 445–444 BC, even though numerous historical sources confirm this date. At this point, what is clear is that neither Anderson's prophetic year calculation nor the solar year calculation dating backward from AD 33 fulfills the 483 years or 69 weeks of years required by Daniel 9:25. Thus, the chronological timeline from the issuing of the decree to rebuild Jerusalem to the first advent of Jesus Christ appears to remain unresolved. Or does it?

It is important to remember that God does not depend on the frailties of chronologists or historians to reveal His truth and glory, especially for the most important events in history—the life, death, and resurrection of our Lord and Savior, Jesus Christ. The Bible reveals that God permanently etched the starting point for the incarnate life and ministry of Jesus in the heavens with a clearly prophesied stellar sign. It was repeatable yet incomparable, naturally occurring yet supernaturally appearing. It has stood the test of time, it fulfills the Scriptures, and significantly, it was not clearly revealed (discovered) until the latter days, just as Daniel prophesied more than 2,500 years ago (Daniel 12:4).

CHAPTER 5

A CHRONOLOGY FOR THE INCARNATE CHRIST: THE HEAVENS DECLARE GOD'S GLORY

God's Heavenly Signs

> The heavens declare the glory of God; the skies proclaim the work of his hands. Day after day they pour forth speech; night after night they display knowledge. There is no speech or language where their voice is not heard. (Psalm 19:1–3 NIV)[1]

From such declaring of God's glory, the proclaiming of His work, the pouring fourth of speech, and the display of knowledge in this passage, it is clear that God's purpose in "stretching out the heavens like a scroll" was not just to provide the sun as a light to rule the day or the moon and stars to rule the night. The glory and wisdom spoken of in this verse was declared from the very beginning, on the fourth day of creation.

And God said, "Let there be lights in the firmament
of the heaven to divide the day from the night; and
let them be for signs, and for seasons, and for days,
and for years. (Genesis 1:14)

The seasons, days, and years in this verse clearly speak of
time and point to the inclusion of heavenly signs for the marking
of important dates and events in God's plan that may have been
missed or misinterpreted by scribes, historians, and chronologists
in the documentation of His history. The word *signs* in this verse
is the same word *(oth)* as used for Cain's "mark" (Genesis 4:15), for
Noah's "token" (meaning the rainbow; Genesis 9:12), for the "great
wonder" in heaven of the woman clothed with the sun (referring
to the constellation Virgo) in Revelation 12:1, and as evidence that
the stars were arranged by God to "signify" something to those on
earth, not just scattered evenly or randomly around in space. Implicit
in this description of heavenly signs is their repeatable nature, even
though such special appearances like the one about to be considered
are extremely rare.

Such is the case for the heavenly sign we call the Bethlehem or
Christmas star that God revealed once, for all time, to mark the birth
of Jesus Christ. We first learn about this seemingly miraculous sign
from Balaam's fourth oracle in the book of Numbers.

I shall see him, but not now; I shall behold him, but
not nigh: There shall come a Star out of Jacob, and
a Sceptre shall rise out of Israel. (Numbers 24:17a)

Dr. Morris comments on this: "This remarkable prophecy of
Balaam anticipates by over 1,400 years the fact that the one who
would hold the scepter (symbolic of kingly rule) over all men would
arise out of Israel, and be announced by a "new" Star displayed in the
heavens *for those who have eyes to see*" (emphasis added).[2]

While the debate continues to this day about whether or not
Balaam's sign was really a star—was it a comet, a supernova, a

one-time appearance of some nonrepeatable stellar event, or even God's Shekinah glory appearing in a cloud or pillar of fire?—the Scriptures are steadfastly clear that this heavenly sign was a star. A first hint in the Old Testament is found in Job 38:6–7.

> Whereupon are the foundations thereof fastened? or who laid the corner stone thereof: When the morning stars sang together and all the sons of God shouted for joy?

Here we see an example of Hebrew parallelism where the "morning stars" were the same as the "sons of God" or angels. Another passage, Isaiah 14:12–13, assigns Satan or Lucifer, the great deceiver, a status synonymous with the stars of heaven.

> How you have fallen from heaven, O morning star, son of the dawn … You said in your heart, I will ascend to heaven; I will raise my throne above the stars of God. (NIV)

In some translations, "morning star" is translated as "day-star." "Lucifer" means "shining one" or "day-star," and here the "stars" are evidently angels (compare Job 38:7). Although Lucifer had a throne as God's "anointed cherub," he aspired to rule over all of God's holy angels.

One might wonder how these passages relate to the Christmas star because they are the only Old Testament passages that reference a star with the same word used in Balaam's oracle—although "Star" in the Numbers passage, along with "Sceptre," is capitalized. If these were the only Scripture passages to link the "Star" sign prophesied by Balaam with the nativity and Christmas star, the case for the heavenly sign being a specific star and not something else might be difficult to prove. It should be noted that the Scriptures do not reveal what additional revelation was given to Daniel, as the "chief of the governors over all the wise men of Babylon" (Daniel 2:48), about the "star" that enabled the wise men to be in Bethlehem on the evening of Jesus's birth when it appeared. Even so, whatever was revealed to these wise men was sufficient for them to be present in Jerusalem on the day of Jesus's birth and to fulfill the prophecies about the star of the nativity. I address this further in this chapter and in detail in *The Christmas Star* (www.thechristmasstar.org).

The Heavenly Sign for Jesus

It may surprise the reader to learn that it is Jesus Christ Himself who confirmed the prophesied heavenly sign to be a specific, special star—at the very end of the Bible. In his revelation to John, nearly sixty years after His death and resurrection, Jesus revealed this.

> I Jesus have sent my angel to give you this testimony for the churches. I am the Root and the Offspring of David and the bright Morning Star. (Revelation 22:16 NIV)

Dr. Morris comments on this verse.

> Satan had aspired to be "Lucifer, son of the morning" (Is 14:12), where "Lucifer" can be translated "Day Star" (Hebrew *haylel),* referring to Venus, the bright star of the dawning. Here, however, after Satan has been forever banished to the lake of fire, Christ proclaims that He alone is "the bright morning star" where "morning" in this case is the Greek *orthoinos,* always referring only to Venus, the star of early dawn. At the end of his revelation, the Lord is reminding all readers that He, not Satan, is the harbinger of eternal light and life. The great conflict of the ages between Satan and Christ, the old serpent and the promised Seed of the woman, will soon be over. Christ is the true Day-Star, Son of the morning.[3]

Of all the observable celestial objects in the heavens, Venus is the only "star" that has ever been referred to (throughout history) as the "bright morning star," the "morning and evening star," or the "day star." Two obvious questions arise that must be answered: (1) If Venus was indeed the Christmas star, how was it possible for a commonly observable planet like Venus to take on an apparent supernatural appearance in order to mark the birth of Christ? (2) Why wasn't it revealed that Jesus is the "bright morning star" until the very end of the Bible, nearly ninety-years after the "star" appeared (Revelation 22:16)?

Applying Daniel's "increased knowledge" that we in this generation now have has made it possible to answer the first question about how it was possible for Venus to be the Nativity star and fulfill the Scriptures. The second question will be addressed at the end of the chapter.

The Bright Morning Star

First question: If Venus was the Christmas star, how is it possible for this familiar and recognizable planet to be transformed into the special star that marked the birth of Jesus Christ?

In Part 1 of *The Christmas Star* (www.thechristmasstar.org), I go into considerable detail about the special qualities and characteristics of Venus that makes it uniquely qualified to be God's special, heavenly sign for the Messiah. Also addressed is how it was possible for the wise men to interpret the other heavenly signs associated with Venus at the time of the nativity and respond to those signs at exactly the right time in order to be in Jerusalem on the day of Jesus's birth. Highlights of the most important reasons why Venus is the only possible stellar candidate to be the Christmas star include the following.

- Venus is the third brightest object in the heavens after the sun and the moon. Depending on sky conditions, Venus can be up to 6.5 times brighter than Jupiter, the fourth brightest object, and 8–10 times brighter than Sirius, the brightest star. Jesus tells us in Revelation 22:16 that He alone is the "bright" morning star. No other star in the heavens has a magnitude of brightness greater than Venus.

- Because Venus is an inner planet, never appearing more than 45 degrees from the sun, it can never be observed at night in the southern sky. Venus is the only stellar object, other than the moon, that can be observed with the naked eye in daylight. This is possible when Venus is separated from the sun by more than about twenty-five degrees in a clear, blue-sky condition. Being able to observe Venus in daylight is a critical aspect of the nativity story that will be explained in the Scripture analysis that follows.

- Many stars we observe as a single star are actually double or multiple stars, even though they appear to the naked eye as a single star. Regulus, Arcturus, Spica, Pollux, and Altair are examples of double stars that always appear to the naked eye as a single star.

- The visible planets (Mercury, Venus, Mars, Jupiter, and Saturn) are unique among heavenly objects because as they travel around the sun along the path astronomers call the ecliptic, they can "temporarily" merge with other visible planets or stars to form a "double star." This merging of planets in close proximity with each other or with a few stars is called a conjunction.

- Because the planets orbit the sun along the same heavenly path at different speeds, conjunctions between planets are fairly common. Normally when planets form a conjunction, they appear as two closely aligned but separate objects to the naked eye because neither has a magnitude of brightness brilliant enough to overpower the other. This is not the case with Venus. With one exception, the brilliance of Venus will normally mask or hide any object, including other planets with which it comes in close contact. The one exception is Jupiter. In the right conditions, especially on a dark, clear night, a conjunction with extremely close separation between Venus and Jupiter can potentially increase the brightness of the resulting merged "double star" by as much as 16 percent. Such an event is extraordinarily rare, but when it happens, Venus, the brightest star in the heavens, can appear to be gloriously bright, just like the "new Star" described by Balaam in Numbers 24:17 or by Jesus as the "bright morning star" in Revelation 22:16.

• Thanks to Johann Kepler's laws of planetary notion and the modern computer, today we have access to more than nine thousand years of Venus-Jupiter conjunction history, past and future. Several parameters are required to determine the significance of such conjunctions, the two most important of which are (1) the separation distance between the two planets when merged and (2) the separation of the conjunction from the sun during the event. While doing Christmas star research, I evaluated all Venus-Jupiter conjunctions for the two hundred years between AD 1900–2100 to determine the significance of separation distance. There are 206 Venus-Jupiter conjunctions during this period, and so a Venus-Jupiter conjunction occurs, on average, about once each year. Four categories of significance, based on separation distance between the planets at the time of the conjunction, were evaluated and are shown below.

Separation distance between Venus and Jupiter for 206 conjunctions between AD 1900–2100[4]

Conjunction Type	Planet Separation (degrees)	Number	Percent
Notable	greater than 1 degree	101	49%
Significant	0.1–1.0 degrees	104	51%
Major	0.01–0.1 degrees	1	0.005%
Extraordinary	less than 0.01 degree	0	0%

As the table reveals, major and extraordinary conjunctions between Venus and Jupiter are extremely rare. When they are visible, all extraordinary conjunctions (less than one one-hundredth of a degree of separation between the planets) will appear to the naked eye as a single star. Many major conjunctions can also appear, at least for a short period of time (in one time zone), as a single star depending on other parameters and sky conditions. The only major conjunction to appear in the current two centuries was on August 27, 2016. What is so significant about the 2016 conjunction is that its parameters were nearly identical to those of the conjunction that gave the wise men the heads-up about the coming Christmas star described in the next paragraphs. More information about the 2016 conjunction is available at **http://thechristmasstar.org/ august-2016-conjunction-and-its-significance.**

Based on what the above data reveal, the next task was to determine how many "extraordinary" conjunctions have ever occurred and when and where they appeared. For this, a review of "Statistical Analysis of 9,400 Years of Venus Jupiter Conjunctions," based on a Solex Program developed by Aldo Vitagliano, was conducted. The analysis revealed that there have only been four Venus-Jupiter conjunctions in all of recorded history that merged to a separation distance of less than one one-hundredth of a degree.

Extraordinary Venus-Jupiter Conjunctions in History[5]

Date	Separation	Elongation	Constellation	Comment
August 8, 3122 BC	0.004 degrees	-18 degrees	Leo	Time of Lamech
August 6, 1128 BC	0.005 degrees	23 degrees	Virgo	Period of Judges
June 17, 2 BC	**0.007 degrees**	**45 degrees**	**Leo**	**Christmas Star**
June 22, 732 AD	0.005 degrees	-18 degrees	Virgo	Post 1st Coming

Data confirm that the only possible candidate for the heavenly sign marking the birth of Jesus Christ was the June 17, 2 BC Venus-Jupiter conjunction—the Christmas star. The 3122 BC conjunction appeared during the time of the patriarchs (Lamech), before the Flood. The 1128 BC appearance was during the time of the Judges, about 100 years before King David. The AD 732 appearance was more than seven hundred years after the birth of Jesus. Importantly, both the 3122 BC and AD 732 AD conjunctions appeared as morning stars, only eighteen degrees from the sun. Thus, they were only visible for the hour just before dawn, but not as "bright" morning stars because it was too light. The 1128 BC conjunction may have been visible longer by about thirty minutes, but the location of this conjunction when it appeared as a single star was in the North American and central and southern Pacific Ocean time zones. With regard to timing, only the June 17, 2 BC conjunction qualifies to be the Christmas star because none of the other extraordinary conjunctions appeared within seven hundred years of the birth of Christ.

The most important facts in support of the June 17, 2 BC, conjunction as the Christmas star, in addition to the parameters and timing of its appearance, are the location where it appeared and the duration of the appearance. This conjunction merged to seven one-thousandths of a degree separation and appeared as the evening star, when Venus was separated from the sun by forty-five degrees, the largest separation distance Venus can have from the sun when observed from the earth. In terms of duration, the conjunction was visible for three full hours after sunset. It appeared in the constellation Leo (the Lion of the tribe of Judah; Genesis 49:9; Revelation 5:5), and most important, it appeared over Israel! In the late afternoon of June 17, about twelve hours after Jesus was born, Venus began to merge with Jupiter high in the southern sky over Jerusalem. By sunset, the two planets were fully merged to within seven one-thousandths of a degree, and for the next three hours Venus was joined with Jupiter as the single, brightest star ever to appear and be recorded in all of history. Moreover, it was visible as a single star across the entire Roman Empire,-from Israel and the Middle East to the Atlantic Ocean. Those with eyes to see would have observed this "once in history" event, but incredibly, it was not recorded in any ancient records—except the Bible.

The Scriptural Evidence

The Scriptures supporting Venus as the Christmas star are found in the Nativity story in Matthew 2. The first reference to the star is verse 2.

> Now when Jesus was born in Bethlehem of Judea in the days of Herod the king, behold, there came wise men from the east to Jerusalem, Saying, "where is he that is born King of the Jews? for *we have seen his star in the east* and are come to worship him." (Matthew 2:1–2; emphasis added).

As it relates to the wise men and the star, an understanding of this verse is the key to the entire Nativity narrative. During the year prior to Christ's birth, another heavenly miracle occurred that brings clarity to this passage that was not known or understood before the twentieth century. Throughout most of the year 3 BC, Venus was the morning star, rising in the east every morning from February to late October, after which it began its transit behind the sun (and thus was not visible) from November until it emerged as the evening star in February 2 BC, five months before the birth of Christ. However, during the Venus transit, ten months before Jesus was born, Venus joined Jupiter when the planets were about twenty-one degrees from the sun to form a major Venus-Jupiter conjunction on August 12, 3 BC (parameters matched the August 27, 2016, conjunction). This was not a "bright" morning star conjunction like the Christmas star, but it was a miraculous appearance in terms of significance, timing, and location. The August 12, 3 BC, "major" morning star conjunction was followed ten months later by the June 17, 2 BC, "extraordinary" evening or Christmas star conjunction. This was an incredible discovery because a search of the 9,400 years of Venus-Jupiter conjunctions reveals that not once in the entire conjunction history data base had two "major" or greater conjunctions ever occurred in back-to-back appearances. Yet here we have a major conjunction in August 3 BC followed ten months later by the most extraordinary Venus-Jupiter conjunction in history. Just as amazing is the fact that both of these major conjunctions were visible (when merged) only over Israel and the surrounding region. The odds for this pair of miraculous appearances to happen back-to-back, are incredible, but for them to both appear and to be observed only over Israel and the surrounding area makes the odds truly astronomical. With God, of course, nothing is impossible.

What makes this discovery so important is that the star the wise men reported they had seen in the east after arriving in Jerusalem (Matthew 2:2) was not the Christmas star. Rather, it was the major conjunction they had seen the previous August. They must have believed the August 12, 3 BC, conjunction was the star that marked the birth of Jesus because it was the first time in more than one thousand years that a major conjunction like it appeared and could have been observed in Israel or elsewhere in the Middle East. It was actually another rare celestial event (a triple conjunction between Jupiter and Regulus) that appeared while Venus was masked by the sun between December 3 BC and February 2 BC, which likely confirmed what they had seen the previous August and prompted the wise men to depart their home in Persia in time to arrive in Jerusalem before the birth of Christ. This is discussed in detail in *The Christmas Star*, but it is what makes possible a literal fulfillment of Scripture for the Nativity narrative.

The wise men must have clearly believed the August 12, 3 BC, conjunction was the Christmas star, and it is what they reported upon their arrival in Jerusalem: "Where is he that is born King of the Jews? … For we have seen his star in the east." This statement caused great concern for Herod and the people. It also created the time required for Herod to inquire of the chief priests and scribes (Matthew 2:3–6) as to where the Christ child was (would be) born, *before* the wise men departed Jerusalem for Bethlehem and the Christmas star actually appeared.

Then Herod, when he had privately called the wise men, inquired of them diligently what time the star appeared. (Matthew 2:7)

At this secret meeting (before Christ was born), the wise men told Herod that the star had appeared ten months earlier in August 3 BC. This makes perfect sense because two months after Jesus's birth, in August 2 BC, after Herod had been mocked by the wise men, he realized that if the child had been born a year earlier, in August 3 BC, he would be at least a year old by then. Thus, he ordered the murder of all the children "from two years old and younger" (Matthew 2:16) in Bethlehem and the surrounding region.

And he sent them to Bethlehem and said, "Go and search diligently for the young child: and when ye have found him, bring me word again, that I may come and worship him also." When they heard the king they departed; and, lo, the star, which they saw in the east, went before them, till it came and stood over where the young child was. When they saw the star, they rejoiced with exceeding great joy. (Matthew 2:8–10)

There are some who believe that the wise men came to Bethlehem as much as two years after Jesus was born. This is obviously not a view supported by Scripture. After the wise men departed Jerusalem following their secret meeting with Herod, the Christmas star appeared that same day! Because this miraculous appearance only happened one time in all of history, the wise men had to make the trip from Jerusalem to Bethlehem on the day of Jesus's birth, when the star appeared. There is no other way to interpret verse 9 as will be made clear in the next paragraphs. The star they had seen in the east on August 12, 3 BC (a Venus-Jupiter conjunction) was exactly the same star that miraculously appeared ten months later on June 17, 2 BC (a Venus-Jupiter conjunction), and it went before them as they traveled to Bethlehem.

Previously, in the facts presented about Venus, I indicated that Venus is the only celestial object other than the moon that can be seen in daylight when its separation is more than about twenty-five degrees from the sun. Venus had been the evening star in the western sky over Israel and around the world since mid-February 2 BC. By late March or early April, when the wise men departed their home in Persia for Israel, Venus was about twelve degrees from the sun, visible for less than an hour after sunset. By May, Venus was separated by thirty to thirty-five degrees from the sun and visible for more than two hours after sunset. In June, by the time the wise men arrived in Jerusalem and before the birth of Christ, Venus reached its maximum separation distance from the sun of forty-five degrees. This means that the wise men literally followed the "bright evening star" from Persia to Jerusalem for their entire westward journey. Importantly, they would also have known where Venus was located in the heavens in daylight.

On the afternoon of June 17, 2 BC (about twelve hours after Jesus's birth), Venus was located high in Jerusalem's southern sky as it began to merge with Jupiter. Bethlehem lies about six miles southwest of Jerusalem, so if the wise men made the journey from Jerusalem to Bethlehem that afternoon, in daylight between 4:00–5:00 p.m., at that time Venus was located high in the southwestern sky, directly ahead of them. Venus could be seen in daylight, separated by forty-five degrees from the sun. Thus, the star they had seen in the east could very well have "gone before them," exactly as described in Scripture. I believe the "exceeding great joy" they experienced was not just at seeing the star in daylight, but it included the realization that they would be visiting a "newborn" child, not a ten-month-old toddler. After the wise men arrived in Bethlehem, Venus "stood" (was stationed in the western sky) as the brightest star to ever appear not just over the place where the "young child was" but over Israel and the rest of the Roman Empire, for the remainder of the evening of June 17, 2 BC.

Historians and chronologists have been debating the details and dates involved in the life and ministry of Jesus Christ for centuries, and the debate will no doubt continue. But one thing is certain: when God stretched out the heavens at the Creation, He put into motion the paths of two planets that would one day appear to merge over a small town in the land of His chosen people to become the greatest, yet least known, repeatable celestial event in all of history—the Christmas star appearance on June 17, 2 BC, which marked the birth of our Savior, the Lord Jesus Christ. From this date, a complete and detailed chronology for the incarnate life, ministry, death, and resurrection of Jesus Christ can be established, and it is in complete harmony with the Scriptures.

Table 6: A Chronology for the Incarnate Life, Ministry, Death, and Resurrection of Jesus Christ

Event	Date	Verse/ Sign
Star the wise men saw in the east	August 12, 03 BC	Matthew 2:2 (major Venus-Jupiter conjunction)
Conception of Jesus Christ (1)	September 11, 03 BC	Matthew 1:20, Luke 1:36 (Rosh Hashana)
Birth of Jesus (absolute date)	**June 17, 02 BC**	Matthew 2:9–10 (the Christmas star)
Circumcision of Jesus	June 25, 02 BC	Luke 2:21 (8th day)
Temple presentation of Jesus (2)	July 27, 02 BC	Luke 2:22; Leviticus 12:5 (> 40th day)
Passover when Jesus was 12 yrs old	March 26, 12 AD	Luke 2:41–42
1st Passover of Jesus's ministry (3)	April 6, 30 AD	Luke 3:23; John 2:13 (30 years old)
2nd Passover of Jesus's ministry (4)	March 27, 31 AD	John 4:3, 5:1, 5:35
3rd Passover of Jesus's ministry (5)	April 13, 32 AD	John 6:4
Palm Sunday (Triumphal Entry (6)	March 29, 33 AD	Matthew 21:1–11; Luke 19:28–48
The Last Supper	April 1, 33 AD	Luke 22:7–18
Crucifixion of Jesus Christ (7)	**April 2–3, 33 AD**	Matthew 28:1 (age: 33 years, 9 months, 16 days)
Resurrection of Jesus Christ	**Sun, April 5, 33 AD**	Luke 24:1
Christ's ascension to heaven	May 15, 33 AD	Acts 1:3
Birth of the Church (Pentecost)	May 25, 33 AD	Acts 2:1

Notes:

Notes 3–7 were edited from Ussher's *Annals of the World*.

1. Some theologians believe Jesus was born during the time of the fall feasts. Based on a June 17, 2 BC, birth date, it is more likely that he was conceived at the time of the fall feasts the previous year. Rosh Hashana, the Feast of Trumpets (1 Tishri), fell on September 11, 3 BC. This was 277 days before the birth of Christ, and it coincides with the human gestation period. Also, the sign of Revelation 12, the virgin (about to give birth) clothed in the sun with the moon at her feet, appeared in the heavens on that date. Significantly, the bright morning star, Venus, was located in the virgin's womb (in the constellation Virgo) during the 3 BC appearance.[6]

2. Luke 2:22 tells us that after the days of Mary's purification were complete (a period of forty days after birth; Leviticus 12:5), his parents took the child to Jerusalem to "present to the Lord." Based on the chronology in Table 6, this event happened after July 27, the fortieth day after Christ's birth. It should be noted that after the visit to Jerusalem for Jesus's dedication, there is no record in Scripture of Jesus ever returning to Bethlehem. Luke 2:39 indicates the family returned to Nazareth, and Matthew 2:13–14 indicates the family fled to Egypt. This means that it would have been impossible for wise men to visit Jesus in Bethlehem during a period from one to two years after the birth, as some claim. Jesus was no longer in Bethlehem and never was again.

3. April 6, 30 AD—The **first Passover (Thursday) and beginning of the ministry of Christ when He was** about thirty years old (Luke 3:23; John 2:13). His age was thirty years, nine months, and nineteen days.[7]

4. March 27, 31 AD—The second Passover (Tuesday) of the ministry of Christ, when He was about thirty-one years old

(John 4:3, 5:1, 5:35). His exact age was thirty-one years, nine months, and nine days.[8]

5. April 14, 32 AD—The third Passover (Monday) of the ministry of Christ, when He was about thirty-two years old (John 6:4). His exact age: thirty-two years, nine months, twenty-seven days.[9]

6. March 29, 33 AD—On Palm Sunday, Jesus entered Jerusalem, descending the Mount of Olives on the colt of an ass **as Messiah the king** (five days before the Passover), when he was about thirty-three years old (Luke 19:28–48). His exact age was thirty-three years, nine months, and eleven days.[10]

7. April 2–3, 33 AD—The **fourth Passover,** in which Christ was sacrificed (Matthew 27:1; 1 Corinthians 5:7) and so put an end to all the legal sacrifices prefiguring this one.[11] Note: While developing this paper, I became aware of the possibility that the Passover date for Jesus's crucifixion may be April 2, not April 3, 33 AD, based on Matthew 12:40. The discussion about this issue is presented in Appendix 3. For the purposes of this chronology, both dates are listed as possible dates for the AD 33 Passover and crucifixion.

Why is the Star not revealed until Revelation?

Why do the Scriptures not reveal Jesus to be the "bright morning star" until the very end of the Bible—nearly ninety years after the star appeared (Revelation 22:16)? In Revelation 22:16, Jesus revealed that He is the "bright morning star" to the churches, but the Church did not exist at the time of his birth, only after his resurrection. I believe the sign was revealed to the Church so that in the latter days, with the increased knowledge spoken of by Daniel, our generation would be able to use the tools of modern astronomy to identify the star and confirm the actual date for Messiah's birth. We must remember that Jesus was hated and persecuted by His generation, as was the Church He created for the next three hundred years.

Neither those in or out of the Church who persecuted Him, nor those who believed in Him were concerned at the time about knowing, promoting, or recording when He was born. God's calendar is not our calendar. He has revealed times and signs to us through the prophets and His Word, including the revelation of a special star to Balaam 1,400 years before it appeared. But God's revelations are for His purposes and glory, not necessarily for illumination at the time they are presented. Whatever He revealed to Daniel and the wise men before the star appeared was sufficient for the wise men to be in Jerusalem on the day of Christ's birth, follow the star to Bethlehem, and fulfill prophecy. Illumination only became possible by modern technology in the latter days.

The world was looking for a sign. The sign appeared, and the whole world missed it. The "bright morning-evening star" has reappeared regularly every few years for the past two thousand years, yet the world remains blind to its truth. This year, 2018, on the 2,019[th] anniversary of Jesus's birth, Venus appeared once again over Bethlehem as the bright evening star. Computer images of the 2 BC Christmas star and the June 2023 "bright evening star" are shown below; the brilliance is not adequately revealed in the computer image. In the first image, Venus and Jupiter are merged, so the Christmas star was significantly brighter than Venus will appear in 2023. Interestingly, when Venus appears on Jesus's birthday in 2023, 2031, and 2039, it will be brighter than it was in 2 BC before and after the conjunction with Jupiter. In 2 BC, Venus had a magnitude of brightness of -4.33. In 2023 it will be -4.36, in 2031 it will be -4.38, and in 2039 it will be -4.41. Venus is and remains the "star" of the Son of God. It appears regularly on His birthday over the place of His birth for His glory, not ours. When will the world have the eyes to see God's glory?

The Christmas Star – 10:15 p.m., June 17, 2 BC, Jerusalem, Israel.[12]

The bright evening star (Venus), 10:08 p.m., June 17, 2023, Jerusalem, Israel.[13]

CHAPTER 6

A BIBLE-BASED CHRONOLOGY
FOR THE SECOND ADVENT
OF JESUS CHRIST

In the previous five chapters, we considered what the Bible reveals about the chronology and timeline of events and people in history, in the past. This chapter will focus on what the Scriptures reveal about the future concerning the chronology and timeline relating to the "time of the end" or "latter days," as prophesied in many passages, including the Daniel 12 passage that began this book and specifically from Christ's own words.

When Will This Time Be?

By His own words, Jesus is coming soon! After Jesus departed the temple and went to the Mount of Olives with His disciples, two days before the feast of Passover, they approached Him privately and asked the three most important questions for all time: (1) When will all this happen? (2) What will be the signs of Your coming? (3) What will be the signs for the end of the world?

And as he (Jesus) sat upon the mount of Olives, the disciples came to him privately, saying, "Tell us, when shall these things be? and what shall be the sign of thy coming, and of the end of the world?" (Matthew 24:3 [1]

The first question they asked was when. In the most detailed answer Jesus gives in the Gospels, He provided a huge clue as to when this time will be, or more precisely when it will start. Implicit in His response was that none of the signs will appear (at least as recognizable birth pangs; Matthew 24:8) before Israel is back in the land. In verse 15, He speaks of the desecration of the third temple (which does not yet exist), and in verse 16 He warned those in Judea to flee to the mountains. Both verses confirm that the Jews are back in the land when the signs Jesus spoke of begin to appear, but not before. The Scriptures are also clear that Israel will be regathered from the four corners of the earth into the land, in a single day, before the signs preceding the end begin to appear as "birth pangs."

This is what the Sovereign Lord says: "Although I sent them far away among the nations and scattered them among the countries, yet for a little while I have been a sanctuary for them in the countries where they have gone.… I will gather you back from the nations and bring you back from the countries where you have been scattered and I will give you back the land of Israel again." (Ezekiel 11:16–17 NIV)[2]

Who has ever heard of such a thing? Can a country be born in a day or a nation be brought forth in a moment? "Do I bring to the moment of birth and not give delivery?" says the Lord. (Isaiah 66:8–9 NIV)[3]

These passages confirm what was prophesied five hundred to seven hundred years before Jesus's birth: that Israel would be reborn in a single day in the land it previously occupied before the signs of the latter days become apparent. That day was May 14, 1948.

An Absolute Date for the start of the Latter Days

In chapter 3, we learned the absolute date of 930 BC from *The Mysterious Numbers of the Hebrew Kings* that linked the two halves of Old Testament history together. In Chapter 5, we learned the absolute date of June 17, 2 BC for the Christmas star that established an accurate chronology for the incarnate life and ministry of Jesus Christ. For the time leading up to the Second Coming of the Messiah based on the "increased knowledge" we have today, spoken of by Daniel, the rebirth of Israel as a nation in a single day marks an absolute date or starting point from which to build a solid, Scripture-based chronology for the period of time we'll define as the latter days. The timelines that follow involve the two centuries between 1900 and 2100, as shown on Timeline 1 below. The span of years will diminish as subsequent prophecies define smaller windows or periods of time.

Timeline 1: The Latter Days

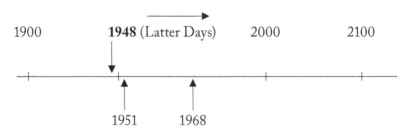

For the latter day timeline, the starting point is the year 1948. The years 1951 and 1968 mark the years when *The Mysterious Numbers of the Hebrew Kings* (1951) was published and when the Christmas star (1968) was discovered, respectively. Both discoveries are in accordance with Daniel's prophecy (Daniel 12:4) that knowledge will increase in the latter days.

The Season of the Lord's Return

The two key Scripture passages that provide the most illumination regarding the timing for the Second Coming are revealed by Jesus in the Olivet Discourse (Matthew 24:30–34; Mark 13:28–31; Luke 21:29–32). In the first, Jesus tells the disciples about the season of His return: "Now learn a parable of the fig tree; when its branch is still tender, and puts forth leaves, know that summer is near" (Matthew 24:32).

The fig tree symbolically represents Israel, as revealed in Jeremiah 8:13, 24:1-7; Hosea 12:2, 9:10; Joel 1:7; and Amos 4:9 in the Old Testament. It's confirmed by the curse Jesus placed on the fig tree, which was representative of Israel in Matthew 21:18–22 and Mark 11:12–14, 20–23. Jesus's curse on the fig tree was a foretelling of God's curse on Israel and its pending destruction and desolation for a time, but not forever. The regathering of the Jews back in the land and the rebirth of the nation in one day (Isaiah 66:8) on May 14, 1948, symbolized the resprouting of the withered fig tree that Jesus cursed. The nation was reborn after 1,878 years—something that has never happened in history to any people or nation.

Many history experts, including Scottish jurist and historian Sir Alex Fraser Tyler (1742–1813) and Ruchir Sharma (author of *The Rise and Fall of Nations*), believe that the average age of the world's great civilizations has been about two hundred year. Online research adds further confirmation that throughout history, the average life-span of a nation has been about two hundred years. From the Truth Project and other Bible-based descriptions, the life cycle of nation can be divided into four main parts: (1) blessings and growth, (2) abundance and a proud heart, (3) forgetting God, and (4) remembrance and repentance—or judgment and destruction. If the two-hundred-year life cycle of a nation is divided into the four seasons, each representing a stage of the nation's life cycle, then we can see how this fits with the parable of the fig tree.

The 200-year Life Cycle of a Nation (Deuteronomy 8:10–20; Hosea 13:6; Revelation 2:5)

Years	Season	Stage of a Nation's Life Cycle
1–50	Spring	Blessings and Growth
51–100	**Summer**	Abundance and a Proud Heart
101–150	Fall	Forgetting God
151–200	Winter	Remembrance and Repentance or Judgment and Destruction

In the fig tree parable, Jesus says of Israel, "When the branch is tender and puts forth leaves, know that that summer is near." In the table above, the summer season represents the period from 51 to 100 years in a nation's life cycle. By applying these numbers to Israel, whose rebirth as a nation was in 1948, Timeline 2 below shows that the 50-year summer season for Israel spans the period of 1998–2048. Today, in 2018, Israel as a nation is 20 years into its 50-year summer season.

Timeline 2: Israel's Summer Season

1948 Spring 1998 **Summer** 2048 Fall 2098 Winter 2148

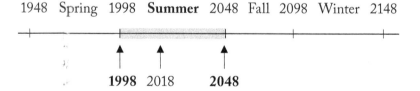

1998 2018 **2048**

Let's consider what the summer season means to religious Jews. It is the season between the spring and fall feasts. Of the seven feasts defined by God in Leviticus 23, the first four (Passover, Unleavened Bread, First Fruits, and Pentecost) take place in the spring season. Most scholars believe the spring feasts were literally fulfilled by Jesus during his first Advent, and the last three feasts (Trumpets, Atonement, and Tabernacles) will be fulfilled during Christ's Second

Coming. The fall feasts are celebrated during the first two weeks of the Jewish civil New Year in the month of Tishri. If the summer season for Israel on the timeline above runs from 1998 to 2048, it may be logical to assume that Christ's return could happen after the year 2048, during the first few years of the fall feast season in Israel's life cycle. But Jesus reveals something in His answer to the disciples' question that should be considered with regard to the timing of his return. In Matthew 24:21–22, Jesus tells us,

> For then there will be great tribulation, such as was not since the beginning of the world to this time, no, nor shall ever be. And except those days should be shortened, there should no flesh be saved: but for the elect's sake, those days shall be shortened. (Matthew 24:21–22)

Because Jesus tells us that "summer is near" in verse 32, the nearness of summer may lead some to believe that "summer" is the heads-up season that immediately precedes the Second Coming, which would occur in the early fall feast season (after 2048). But, Jesus tells us in verse 22 that the seven-year tribulation will be so horrific that if it continued, "no flesh would be saved." He confirms that the time just prior to His return is so bad that "those days will be shortened." Thus, although it may be possible to make a scriptural case for the Second Coming happening in the season of early fall (after 2048), the shortening of days Jesus tells us will happen would logically push the time of the Second Coming back into the summer season. How far back we cannot know, but without additional revelation about the timing, at this point we will define the "Season of the Lord's return" as the fifty-year "summer season of Israel as a nation" between 1998 and 2048. In 2018, Israel's summer season is in its twentieth year.

An interesting discovery was made while doing the above analysis, and because it may shed light on the timing of the Messiah's return, I will share it here. Israel's four seasons as a nation include the two fifty-year periods representing the spring and fall feasts. For those who believe Christ's return will happen during the fall feasts in whatever season it occurs, there is a clear scriptural basis for this. Assuming His return is during Israel's summer season, it is very probable it will happen during the fall feasts in whatever year(s) He returns. Jesus fulfilled the requirements for each of the spring feasts in April and May 33 AD to the very day (Unleavened Bread, April 1; Passover, April 2–3; First Fruits, April 5; Pentecost, May 25), and so it is not unreasonable to believe that He will fulfill the three fall feasts (Trumpets = Rapture; Atonement = Second Coming; Tabernacles = Millennial Kingdom) at those times in whatever year(s) these events take place.

What I discovered was this: the Lord's birthday on June 17 (from chapter 5) falls almost exactly between the spring and fall feasts. The spring feasts begin each year after the March 21–22 vernal equinox, and the fall feasts normally begin during the first eleven days of September (1 Tishri on the Hebrew calendar). There can be nine days in March, sixty-one days in April and May, and sixteen days in June for a total of eighty-six days, after the start of the spring feasts, before Jesus's June 17 birthday. There are thirteen days in June, there are sixty-two days in July and August, and there can be eleven days in September for a total of eighty-six days after his birthday, before the start of the fall feasts. The fact that Jesus's birthday falls almost exactly in middle of the period between the spring and fall feasts may be coincidental. But then, with God there is no such thing as coincidence.

The Generation That Will See All These Things

The third part of Jesus's answer to the disciple's question about when these things will be relates to the period of a generation.

> I tell you the truth, this generation will not pass away until all these things have happened. (Matthew 24:34 NIV)

In context, Jesus told the disciples that there is a specific generation that will see all the signs He described in His answer to their question, and that the generation will not pass away until everything prophesied by the signs, including His return, is fulfilled. Two questions that arise are (1) How long is a generation, and (2) What specific generation is Jesus talking about?

There has been much speculation about the length of a generation even to this day, with the most recent length being postulated in *The Coming Convergence* (2017) as being 80–120 years.[4] But there is only one verse in the Bible that defines the length of a generation: Psalm 90:10.

> The days of our years are threescore and ten (70);
> and if by reason of strength they be fourscore [80]
> years, yet is their strength labor and sorrow, for it is
> soon cut off, and we fly away.

This is a psalm of Moses, a prayer of the man of God, titled "Teach Us to Number Our Days." Although Moses lived longer, the passage was not written in reference to himself. Dr. Morris has this to say about the verse: "Moses contrasts the normal span of 70 years in his day (even though he himself lived 120 years) with the thousand-year life-span of men before the flood (90:4). It is remarkable that, after 3,000 years of human history after Moses, including the great medical advances of recent centuries, 70–80 years is still the normal lifespan."[5]

We learn much about how God defined a generation from the Exodus story. A major reason why Moses led the Israelites in the wilderness for forty years was to ensure that none of those who departed Egypt in the Exodus, over the age of twenty years, would remain alive to enter the Promised Land as punishment for being a "stiff necked" people (Numbers 14:28–29). Thus with the exceptions of Joshua and Caleb, all who entered the Promised Land after forty years in the wilderness were sixty years or younger in age. After the death of Moses, there are only three references in the Bible to people older than eighty years of age. Joshua 14:7–10 reveals that Caleb was eighty-five years old when he was given his inheritance. In 1 Samuel 4:15, the priest, Eli, was ninety-eight years old when he died. In Luke 2:36–38, the eighty-four-year-old temple prophetess Anna is described as "a woman of a great age" when she praised and gave thanks to the Lord at the dedication of the baby, Jesus. Daniel, who went into the Babylonian captivity as a teenager and lived through the entire period, probably died between the ages of eighty-five and ninety. Kings David and Solomon lived to seventy years, and Uzziah and Manassah, the longest reigning kings in Judah, lived to seventy-seven and seventy-eight years, respectively. These examples span a period of nearly 1,500 years of Old Testament history, and they clearly support the length of a generation as revealed in Psalm 90:10 to be a period of seventy to eighty years.

The Psalm 90:10 prophecy also supports our life expectancy in the modern era (time of the latter days). The most recent US census age demographic data (2016)[6] reveals that today, only about 2 percent of Americans live to see their eighty-first birthday. This means that fewer than three out of every one hundred people born in 1937 remain alive today. Thus the Scriptures and current US census data jointly confirm the length of a generation to be seventy to eight years, as defined by Moses in Scripture 3,500 years ago.

In the Exodus story, God divided the eighty-year life span of a generation into four segments or age groups. Each segment was twenty years in length based on that generation's ability to reproduce the next generation.

Age	Definition
0–20 years	Pre-productive years
21–40 years	Productive years (reproduction years)
41–60 years	Productive years
61–80 years	Post-productive years

At the time of the Exodus, four generations (twenty years in each generation) departed Egypt, but only three generations were allowed to enter the Promised Land. This is because those over twenty years old when they left Egypt died in the wilderness. Only those under twenty at the Exodus and the two generations born during the forty-year period of wandering were allowed to enter the land. From the census taken by Moses at the end of the forty years in the wilderness and before entering the Promised Land, there were 603,550 men of war aged twenty-one to sixty (Numbers 1:45–46). If we assume an equal population of adult women (600,000) and an equal population distribution among the three age groups (pre-productive population = 600,000), the total population of the Jews at the time they entered Canaan would have been about 1.8 million people.

We also know that God revealed exactly who the Exodus generation was. Only one group of Jews who lived during a specific twenty-year period experienced all that happened in the Exodus—the plagues, the Exodus, forty years in the wilderness, and entering, conquering, and settling the Promised Land. It was the pre-productive group, aged one to twenty years, who were alive at the time of the Exodus. We know from Table 5 in chapter 3 that the Exodus was in 1446 BC. Therefore the Exodus generation that experienced "all those things" was born during the twenty-year period between 1466 and 1446 BC.

Today, there are four generations, with each generally defined by a twenty-year period: baby boomers, generation X, generation Y, and generation Z (millennials). Many once believed the World War II (Greatest) generation, who saw the rebirth of Israel as a nation, was the generation that "would see all these things." But today the youngest surviving members of that generation are in their nineties, more than a decade beyond the eighty-year span of a generation prophesied by Moses. The generation that most closely coincides with the rebirth of Israel as a nation is the baby boomer generation. For this analysis, the year 1948 will mark the center point of the twenty-year period between 1938 and 1958. This twenty-year period includes ten years on either side of 1948, the year of Israel's rebirth. Because the period does not coincide exactly with baby boomer years and is not the "terminal" generation (three subsequent generations are alive today), the generation centered on the year 1948 (Israel's rebirth) that was born between 1938 and 1958 is identified for our purposes as the "witness" generation. If Jesus's prophecy (Matthew 24:34) for the generation that would "see all these things" was meant to include those alive who would see Israel's rebirth as a nation, then the first ten years of our defined witness generation (1938–1948) includes those who would potentially see "all these things" from the rebirth of Israel to the Second Coming of Jesus Christ. The second half, those born between 1949 and 1958 were not alive to see Israel's rebirth, but they would see and experience all the other signs prophesied for the latter days.

A witness born in 1948 turned seventy years old (with Israel) in 2018 and began his or her final decade before "passing away" after turning eighty in 2028. Timeline 3 below shows how the witness born in 1948 matches with the timeline for the rebirth of Israel in 1948. The culminating timeline will include the entire twenty-year witness generation for the period from 1938 to 1958.

Timeline 3: A Witness Born in 1948

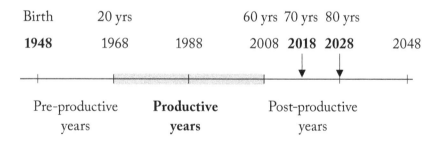

It is interesting that the forty-year productive period for the person born in 1948 spans the period from 1968 to 2008. A significant number of the end-time signs prophesied by Jesus and the prophets have appeared and even converged during this period. The timeline for the productive years for the whole witness generation (1938–1958) is truly remarkable. For a person born in 1938, the productive years are 1958 to 1998. For a person born in 1958, they are 1978 to 2018. The total productive year period for the generation born between 1938 and 1958 is the sixty-year period between 1958 and 2018. This period encompasses virtually all the signs prophesied to appear and converge before Christ returns.

How Does the Rapture fit in the End-time Chronology?

The first part of Christ's Second Coming will be the rapture of the Church (1 Thessalonians 4; 1 Corinthians 15), when Jesus returns in the air to "snatch away" His saints from the earth "before the wrath to come." Revelation 3:10 defines a gap in time between the Rapture and the Second Coming: "Because thou hast kept the word of my patience, I will also keep thee from the hour of temptation, which shall come upon all the world, to try them that dwell upon the earth."

Dr. Morris has this to say about the timing between the Rapture and the Second Coming of Christ.

> This "hour of temptation" was yet to "come upon all the world," so this statement could not have referred to any events of the first century. Its purpose will be "to try them that dwell upon the earth." It is a time of judgment on unbelievers, not on believers. This testing will be "the great day of his wrath" (Rev 6:17), the seven-year period of tribulation at the end of the age (Da 9:27; Ma 24:15–21). God has promised to deliver all true believers from this "hour of temptation" (or testing), for "God hath not appointed us to wrath, but to obtain salvation by our Lord Jesus Christ" (1 Th 5:9). This passage clearly teaches that the resurrection and rapture of true Christian believers must take place before the hour of temptation (seven-year tribulation) begins (1 Th 4:16–17).[7]

This means that there will be at least seven years of time separation (to accommodate the seven-year tribulation) between the Rapture and the Second Coming. There is no prophesied sign that requires fulfillment for the Rapture to happen. The Rapture has been an imminent event (meaning it will happen suddenly) since the prophecy was written by Paul. It will happen in the twinkling of an eye with no warning. The only time reference we have for the Rapture is that it will happen before the seven-year tribulation period that marks the end of the age and the Second Coming of Jesus Christ, although Scripture provides some clues. One view holds that the tribulation will begin shortly (within a year or two) after the Rapture because the restraining force (presence of the Holy Spirit in the Church) that keeps the world from descending into chaos will be removed (2 Thessalonians 2:3–7). Prophecy expert Gary Stearman adds this: "Another view held by many serious dispensational prophecy researchers is that the rapture will come about three, four or more years before the tribulation, in part because the start of the Gog-Magog war, described in Ezekiel 38:18–20, appears to be linked to the beginning of the tribulation and it requires some time to develop."[8]

Timeline 4 below is based on the premise that the Rapture takes place before the tribulation. The long arrow represents the immanency of the Rapture as the pending event moves forward through time, with the arrow's point representing the specific event when it happens. As the pending Rapture event moves forward through time, it pushes the seven-year tribulation period ahead of it. The space between the arrow point and the tribulation, in brackets, is undefined. But in consideration of the views expressed above, we can assume the space or gap between the Rapture event and start of the tribulation is a period of between one and five years, which means the Rapture will most likely happen from seven to twelve years before Christ's Second Coming.

Timeline 4: The Rapture Timeline

Rapture

(time) ──────────────────────► (7-year Tribulation)

2018

I want to briefly comment on a Barna study done in 2001 because it may have a direct bearing on the number of American Christians who will actually be raptured, depending on the timing of the event. The Bible is clear that there will be a "falling away from the faith" and "Godlessness" in the latter days (1 Timothy 4:1; 2 Timothy 3:1–6). The 2001 Barna study revealed that only about 9 percent of American evangelicals were believed to have a "Christian worldview" based on seven specific questions posed to a large demographic database. An often overlooked point made in the study was that the percentage of those in the American population holding a Christian worldview had been dropping at an average rate of about 4 percent per decade during the previous four decades, and the study predicted that the trend would continue.[9] This means that starting in 1961, the number of Americans holding a Christian worldview has steadily declined as follows: 1961, 25 percent; 1971, 21 percent; 1981, 17 percent; 1991, 13 percent; and 2001, 9 percent. Based on this trend, the future projection looks like this: 2011, 5 percent; 2021, 1 percent. The current percentage in 2018 would be about 2.2 percent.

What follows is purely speculation, but it might provide insight regarding God's plan and timing for the Rapture. The Bible is clear that only true believers (God alone knows each heart) will be raptured. For example, if we assume those in the American population with a Christian worldview represent the number most likely to be raptured, then based on the above percentages from the Barna study, the raptured population might look something like this if the event occurred in a given year: 1961, 50 million; 1981, 47 million; 1991, 38 million; 2001, 27 million; 2011, 15.3 million;

2018, 6.8 million; and 2021, 3.15 million. Although these numbers may not be accurate, the trend is unmistakably clear. By 2031, the number drops to less than 1.3 million. If the projection is even remotely accurate, then if our "blessed hope" doesn't return to claim His living saints before the year 2041, there may be fewer than one million true believing American Christians who will be raptured.

Bringing It All Together: A Latter Day Prophetic Timeline

From what is presented above, we can draw the following Bible-based conclusions about Jesus's answer to the disciples' question: "When shall these things be?"

- We cannot know the day or the hour of the Lord's return (Matthew 24:36).
- The latter days began at the rebirth of Israel as a nation on May 14, 1948 (Isaiah 66:8).
- The summer season for the Lord's return is the fifty-year period between 1998 and 2048 (Matthew 24:32).
- The final two decades (seventy to eighty years; Psalm 90:10) of the witness generation (those born between 1938 and 1958) that will most likely "see all these things" before passing away is the twenty-year period between 2018 and 2038 (Matthew 24:34).
- The Rapture is an imminent, signless event that will most likely happen between one to five years before the Tribulation begins (1 Thessalonians 4; 1 Corinthians 15) and thus will occur seven to twelve years before the Second Coming of Jesus Christ.

By combining the timelines for the three-part answer to the question "when," given by the Lord to His disciples—the start of the latter days, the season of the Lord's return, the last twenty years of the witness generation, and the Rapture event—we have Timeline 5, shown below.

Timeline 5: The Witness Generation Timeline

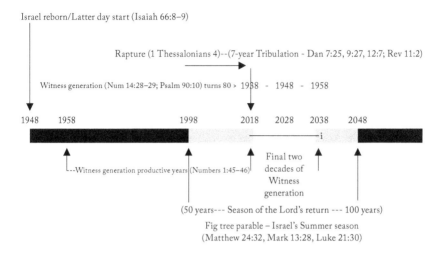

Israel reborn/Latter day start (Isaiah 66:8–9)

Rapture (1 Thessalonians 4)--(7-year Tribulation - Dan 7:25, 9:27, 12:7; Rev 11:2)

Witness generation (Num 14:28–29; Psalm 90:10) turns 80 > 1938 - 1948 - 1958

1948   1958   1998   2018   2028   2038   2048

--Witness generation productive years (Numbers 1:45–46)   Final two decades of Witness generation

(50 years--- Season of the Lord's return --- 100 years)

Fig tree parable – Israel's Summer season
(Matthew 24:32, Mark 13:28, Luke 21:30)

Key to the Witness Generation Timeline

1. Israel's rebirth in 1948 marks the start of the latter days timeline (Isaiah 66:8–9).
2. The black segment of the timeline prior to 1998 represents the spring season (years 1–50) for the nation of Israel. The black segment after the year 2048 represents the first years of the fall season (years 101–150) for Israel as a nation.
3. The Rapture is an imminent, pending event presently moving day by day through the year 2018. It pushes the seven-year Tribulation period ahead of it. The Rapture can happen at any moment, especially now that it has entered the unshaded "white zone," or the final two decades of the witness generation in 2018 (John 14:1–3; 1 Thessalonians 4:13–18; 1 Corinthians 15:51–54).
4. The witness generation includes those born during the twenty-year period between 1938 and 1958. In 2018, the witness generation begins to pass away as those born in 1938 turn eighty years old. When those born in 1958 turn eighty

in 2038, the witness generation will have effectively "passed away" (Numbers 14:28–29; Psalm 90:10).

5. The productive years for the witness generation are the sixty-year period between 1958 and 2018. (Numbers 1:45–46). This is the period when all the signs prophesied by Jesus should "appear" and "converge." The increase in frequency and intensity of these end time signs will continue into the Tribulation.

6. The season of the Lord's return is Israel's summer season (Matthew 24:32; Mark 13:28; Luke 21:30). This is the fifty-year period between 1998 and 2048. It is highlighted in gray on the timeline above, and it marks the most probable window of time for the Lord's return. The year 2018 marks the twentieth year of Israel's summer season, the seventieth year of reborn Israel as a nation, and the seventieth birthday for a person born in 1948.

7. The final two decades of the witness generation is the twenty-year period between 2018 and 2038. It includes the eightieth year (Psalm 90:10) for everyone born in the witness generation and is highlighted by the unshaded segment on the timeline. If this truly is the generation that "will not pass away" before all takes place as spoken of by Jesus, then the most probable window of time for the Second Coming is the period of time between about 2026 (assuming the seven-year tribulation period begins within a year or two of 2018) and 2038.

Does God Have a Seven-Thousand-Year Plan for His Creation?

The Bible-based chronology developed in this book reveals an age since the Creation of 6,132 years (as of 2018). In view of this, I thought it might be interesting to see how this chronology fits with what some believe to be God's seven-thousand-year plan as revealed in Scripture. The key verses that apply include the following.

Lord, thou hast been our dwelling place in all generations. Before the mountains were brought forth, or ever thou hast formed the earth and the world, even from everlasting to everlasting, thou art God... For a thousand years in thy sight are but yesterday when it is past, and as a watch in the night. (Psalm 90:1–2, 4)

But, beloved, be not ignorant of this one thing, that one day is with the Lord as a thousand years, and a thousand years as one day. (2 Peter 3:8)

And he laid hold on the dragon, that old serpent, which is the Devil, and Satan, and bound him for a thousand years ... And I saw the thrones and they sat upon them, and judgment was given to them; and I saw the souls of them that were beheaded for the witness of Jesus, and for the word of God, and which had not worshipped the beast, neither his image, neither had received his mark upon their foreheads or in their hands, and they lived and reigned with Christ a thousand years ... But the rest of dead lived not again until the thousand years were finished ... And when the thousand years are expired, Satan shall be loosed out of his prison. (Revelation 20:2, 4–5, 7)

Many interpret these prophesies literally, believing that because God created everything from nothing in six literal days and rested on the seventh, the seven days of creation prophetically represent seven thousand years of human history on the earth. The first six thousand years covers the period from the Creation to Christ's Second Coming, and the final thousand years represent the thousand-year millennial kingdom. Second Peter 3:8 seems to support this interpretation, and the Revelation 20 verses clearly support a millennial kingdom of one thousand years in length. If true, and our chronology shows that 6,132 years have already elapsed since the creation, is it still possible to support a literal six-thousand-year period between the creation and the Second Coming of Christ as a part of God's seven-thousand-year plan?

The analysis that follows is a bit unusual because most who have written about this issue either assume the six thousand years since the Creation has not yet transpired, or they define significant periods of time or ages with gaps that may be difficult to support scripturally. I will approach this issue in the belief that if the chronology for the 6,132 years from the Creation to 2018 (in Table 7) is a true reflection of God's plan, then we should be able to use major times, people, and events revealed in Scripture to confirm over 6,132 years of history, with scripturally supportable gaps, if required.

To do this, it is worthwhile to consider the people and events in the chronology that most strongly magnify and glorify God's plan and purposes. Our starting point is the Creation itself, because without it nothing (including humanity) would exist. The end point is the Second Coming of Christ. Between these end points, we currently have 6,132 years of elapsed history, and Christ has not yet returned. Many have divided the six thousand years prior to the millennium into three fairly equal two-thousand-year segments. That is what we will do, because I believe there are two personages and events that surpass all others in history when considered from God's perspective (if that is even possible).

The most significant and important event after the Creation was the incarnate life, ministry, death, and resurrection of Jesus Christ. Without His sacrifice on the cross for our redemption, there would be no hope and no purpose for life. The Christ's incarnate life spanned nearly thirty-four years from 2 BC to AD 33.

I believe the second most important or precious thing to God is the "apple of His eye," His chosen people, Israel. Israel would not exist without the faithful walk of God's servant and friend Abraham and the Abrahamic Covenant. Abraham's life spanned 175 years from 2166 to 1991 BC.

Let's see what the first six thousand of years of God's seven-thousand-year plan looks like if we consider how these two lives fit between the Creation and the Second Coming end points. The period from the Creation to Abraham includes the worldwide flood and has been referred to by some as the Age of Chaos. Abraham was born 1,948 years after the creation and so was 52 years old in the 2,000th year after the Creation. If the Creation was in 4114 BC, then two thousand years later, Abraham turned fifty-two in 2114 BC:

Creation to Abraham's 52nd year—**2,000 years**—4114–2114 BC

Jesus Christ was born in 2 BC. Two thousand years earlier, in 2002 BC, Abraham was still alive and was 164 years old. The time between Abraham and Jesus can be referred to as the Age of Israel (God's chosen people).

Abraham to Jesus Christ—**2,000 years**—2002 BC–2 BC

Jesus Christ died and was resurrected in the year AD 33. Five weeks after His resurrection was Pentecost and the birth of the Church, beginning the Church Age or the Age of Grace. The two thousandth anniversary of Christ's death and resurrection and the birth of the Church is in AD 2033.

Resurrection and Pentecost to 2,000th
anniversary—**2,000 years**—AD 33–2033 AD

If we put these events and dates on a timeline, they neatly fit within the Table 7 chronology (below) to fulfill the first six thousand years of God's seven-thousand-year plan:

Timeline 6: God's Seven-thousand-year Plan

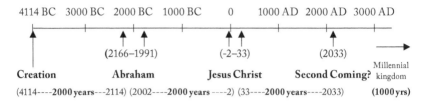

It should be noted that there was no year zero. This timeline works for God's seven-thousand-year plan even though the Second Coming has not yet happened. The two thousandth anniversary of the Church in 2033 clearly fits with a Second Coming event during the twenty-year final decade period between 2018 and 2038 for the witness generation, shown in Timeline 5. In 2018, fifteen years remain before the third segment reaches two thousand years. Only if the Second Coming happens after AD 2033 will the third two-thousand-year segment begin to increase in length. With this timeline, the only gaps in the six-thousand-plus year period involve portions of Jesus's and Abraham's life spans. There are 112 years of Abraham's lifetime between the first two two-thousand-year segments and the thirty-four years spanning Jesus's lifetime between the second and third two-thousand-year segments. Therefore, God's seven-thousand-year plan can be supported by Scripture and the Bible-based chronology as revealed in Table 7 below. Table 7 is a compilation of the chronologies from Tables 1, 2, 4, 5, and 6.

Table 7: A Complete Bible-Based Chronology from the Creation to the Second Advent of Christ

A. Chronology for the Period from the Creation to Artaxerxes' Decree

Person/Event	AC date(s)	BC date(s)
The Creation	0	4114 BC
Birth of Noah	1056 AC	3058 BC
The Genesis Flood	1656 AC	2458 BC
Death of Noah	2006 AC	2108 BC
Life of Abraham	1948–2123 AC	2166–1991 BC
Birth of Jacob	2108 AC	2006 BC
Start of Israel's sojourn in Egypt	2238 AC	1876 BC
The Exodus	2668 AC	1446 BC
Aaron's death; end 40 years in wilderness	2708 AC	1406 BC
Birth of David	3074 AC	1040 BC
Death of David; Solomon king	3144 AC	970 BC
Seven yr construction of the first temple	3148–3155 AC	966–959 BC
Dedication of the first Temple	3155 AC	959BC
Solomon's death; divided kingdom	3184 AC	930 BC
Hoshea, last king of Israel	3382–3391 AC	732–723 BC
Destruction of Israel by the Assyrians	3391 AC	723 BC
Josiah reign	3474–3505 AC	640–609 BC
Jehoiakim reign	3505–3516 AC	609–598 BC
Nebucudnezzar's siege; 70-year captivity	3509 AC	605 BC
Jerusalem besieged; king taken captive	3517 AC	597 BC
Jerusalem fell; temple destroyed	3528 AC	586 BC
Decree by Cyrus ending captivity	3582–3581 AC	538–537 BC
Period of 70-year Babylonian captivity	3509–3579 AC	605– 535 BC
Period of 70-year Temple desolation	3528-3599 AC	586-515 BC
Completion of 2nd temple under Darius I	3599 AC	515 BC
Esther rises to queen of Persia	3628 AC	478 BC
Artaxerxes decree to rebuild Jerusalem	3670 AC	444 BC

See notes 1–7 on Table 5 (end of chapter 3).

B. Chronology for the Incarnate Period of the Life and Ministry of Jesus Christ

Event	Date
Star the wise men saw in the east	August 12, 03 BC
Conception of Jesus Christ (1)	September 11, 03 BC
Birth of Jesus (absolute date)	**June 17, 02 BC**
Circumcision of Jesus	June 25, 02 BC
Temple presentation of Jesus (2)	July 27, 02 BC
Passover when Jesus was 12 yrs old	March 26, 12 AD
1st Passover of Jesus's ministry (3)	April 6, 30 AD
2nd Passover of Jesus's ministry (4)	March 27, 31 AD
3rd Passover of Jesus's ministry (5)	April 13, 32 AD
Palm Sunday (Triumphal Entry) (6)	March 29, 33 AD
The Last Supper	April 1, 33 AD
Crucifixion of Jesus Christ (7)	**April 2–3, 33 AD**
Resurrection of Jesus	**Sun, April 5, 33 AD**
Christ's ascension to heaven	May 15, 33 AD
Birth of the Church (Pentecost)	May 25, 33 AD

See notes 1–7 on Table 6 (end of chapter 5).

C. The Period of the Latter Days from Israel's Rebirth to the Second Advent of Jesus Christ

Event	Date/year	Verse(s)
First birth year of the witness generation	1938	
Re-birth of Israel as a nation	May 14, 1948	*Absolute date*
Beginning year of the Latter Days	1948	*Is 66:8-9, Ez 11:16-17*
Final birth year of the witness generation	1958	
First Productive year of the witness generation	1958	*Numbers 1:45-46*
Beginning of Israel's Summer season as a nation	1998	*Matthew 24:34*
Final Productive year of the witness generation	2018	
Witness generation begins 20 period of "passing away"	2018	*Psalm 90:10*
(Christ's Return Part 1 – The Rapture)	??	
Passover -2,000th anniversary of Christ's crucifixion	April 14, 2033	*hebcal.com*

Pentecost- 2,000th anniversary of birth of the Church	June 3, 2033	*hebcal.com*
(Christ's Return – The Second Coming)	??	Psalm 90:10, Ma 24:36
Final year of the witness generation's passing away	2038	Matthew 24:34
Final year of Israel's Summer season as a nation	2048	

Notes:

1. The latter day chronology assumes the witness generation begins passing away in 2018 and has passed away by the end of 2038. If this indeed is the timeframe for the generation that "will see all these things" before it passes away, then:

2. The most probable timeframe for the rapture to occur (first part of the Second Coming - a sign-less event), is between the years 2018 and 2031 (the next 12 years), in order for the seven year tribulation and Christ's return to take place before the end of 2038 when the witness generation has "passed away".

3. The most probable timeframe for the Second Coming, which requires several Bible prophesies to be fulfilled (e.g. revealing of the Antichrist, the third temple, the seven year tribulation), if the rapture were to happen as soon as 2019, would be between the years 2026-2038, before the witness generation has "passed away".

4. This chronology assumes that the rapture, the tribulation and the Second Coming will all take place in the 20 year period between 2018 and 2038, by which time the witness generation that has seen all these things will have passed away.

Conclusion

Developing this book was an amazing, spirit-filled journey. The premise from the outset was that God told Daniel to seal up the books until the time of the end, when knowledge would increase (Daniel 12:4), and we would finally understand God's timeline and know the latter days were upon us when the end-time prophecies could be understood and were being fulfilled. An important reason why I believe we are in that time today is because none of the three "absolute dates" that enabled a complete and accurate Bible chronology, revealed in this book, were possible to determine before Israel was back in the land in 1948.

Who could have known, for instance, that Judah alone, among all its ancient neighbors including Israel, reckoned years (in Scripture) from Tishri to Tishri as opposed to Nisan to Nisan, in direct opposition to God's guidance to Moses (Exodus 12:1). It wasn't until after Israel was back in the land, the Hebrew language was restored, and the Jewish civil calendar dating from Tishri to Tishri was resumed that the discovery was made. All the dates and chronologies existed in the Masoretic text for more than 2,500 years, but God allowed the "mysterious numbers of the Hebrew kings" to remain a mystery until efforts like those of Dr. Edwin Thiele uncovered the truth in the late 1940s. In 1951, his revelation of an absolute date (930 BC) for the divided kingdom enabled chronologies dating from the Creation to the divided kingdom, and from the divided kingdom forward, to finally be linked and understood, as revealed in chapter 3.

Today, after more than two thousand years, it is hard to imagine how the most important birthday in all of history, the birth of Jesus Christ, has been hidden from our eyes for so long. God laughed and scoffed (Psalm 2:4) while man vainly attempted for two millennia to identify this important date, based almost exclusively on when the wicked King Herod died. Herod's death did fulfill prophecy in that he did not die, nor did the Scepter depart from Judah, until after the Messiah was born (Genesis 49:10; Matthew 2:19). Some historians have attempted to link Christ's birth to heavenly signs, particularly solar and lunar eclipses, but only with respect to a date for the death of Herod. This is because until the 1960s and the development of computer programming, it was impossible to know what glory the heavens truly reveal about the past. Before Israel's rebirth, historical claims about heavenly signs and unique stellar configurations referred almost exclusively to comets and lunar and solar eclipses. In doing Christmas star research, I could not find a single historical reference to a planetary conjunction, which is the only naturally occurring source of a "new" albeit temporary star like the one that marked the birth of Christ.

God chose the two most commonly observed stars (planets) in the heavens, Venus and Jupiter, to come together in a rare and particular way, over a particular location, and at one specific time in all of recorded history to forever mark the birth date of our Lord and Savior, Jesus Christ. Only after the laws of planetary motion were applied to computer software in the 1960s (after Israel's rebirth) was it possible to accurately determine when Jesus was born. Thus, the second absolute date for the birth of Jesus, June 17, 2 BC, has been established (chapter 5). With a reliable birth date for Christ, a solid, Scripture-based chronology for Jesus's life and ministry can be confirmed.

The third absolute date, in chapter 6, was the simplest to determine. Isaiah 66:8–10 reveals that Israel would be reborn as a nation in a single day and thus begin the latter days and the final countdown to the Second Coming of Jesus Christ. That absolute date was May 14, 1948. This year, 2018, marks the seventieth year since the countdown began. Although we do not know the exact day or hour of His return, Jesus's own words clearly reveal enough so that we "children of light" might know and be prepared for what is coming, exactly as Daniel, the other prophets, and the New Testament writers prophesied.

From the parable of the fig tree, Israel's summer season for the Lord's return necessarily becomes the fifty-year period between 1998 and 2048. The witness generation comprises those born starting a decade before Israel's rebirth in 1938 and includes those born in the decade following Israel's rebirth until 1958, so that some in that generation would be alive for the rebirth of Israel. Others would see and experience all the prophesied signs requiring fulfillment and convergence before the Second Coming. Importantly, some in the witness generation will live to see Israel's rebirth *and* the fulfillment of all the signs. The "productive years" of the witness generation is the sixty-year period between 1958 and 2018. This is not just the period when all the end-time signs have been prophesied to appear and converge, but it is actually the witness generation who contributes most directly to the development and appearance of many of the signs. Finally, the oldest members of the witness generation (those born in 1938) turn eighty years old in 2018 to begin the twenty-year "passing away" period that ends when those born in 1958 effectively pass away in 2038. If this truly is the generation described by Jesus—and I believe it is—then the witness generation will not completely pass away before Christ returns, just as revealed in Scripture by Jesus Himself (Matthew 24:34).

The Rapture has always been an imminent event, but in 2018 it became a pending, looming, imminent event. All the windows of time described in chapter 6 converge to mark this time as the beginning of the final two decades of the countdown to Christ's return. Timeline 5 reveals 2018 to be the year when all the arrows converge and point to a "red zone," the final twenty-year period described in Jesus's own words as the beginning of the "passing away" of a specific end-time generation. Everything appears to be lining up for the fulfillment of God's plan, but despite what has been presented, we cannot know exactly when Jesus will return to rapture His Church. We can, however, be confident that the Second Coming will take place seven to twelve years after the Rapture. The Scriptures and the windows of time that have been developed seem to illuminate a window of time starting seven to twelve years from now (2025–2030) and lasting until the year 2038 (when the witness generation finally passes away) as the most probable window of time for all the end-time prophecies (including the Second Coming) to be fulfilled. The year 2033 is especially interesting because it marks the two thousandth anniversary year of Christ's crucifixion and resurrection and the birth of the Church, and it fits with God's seven-thousand-year timeline described in chapter 6. Fortunately for true believers, including this writer, we are not looking for the Second Coming. We await and anticipate the return of our blessed hope at the Rapture. It's the day, the moment, when the Lord returns in the air to bring all His saints (those who have put their faith and trust in Him), both those who have "fallen asleep" and those still alive, home to be with Him. Thus, it is clear that now is the time to proclaim to the world with great confidence that Jesus is coming soon!

This book does not address specific end-time signs that have appeared and converged these past sixty years—signs that should open eyes, ears, and hearts to the nearness of the Lord's return—in part because there are so many and because the specific signs were not the book's focus. That said, I want to conclude by considering one positive sign that spanned the entire sixty-year productive period (1958–2018) of the witness generation. Dr. Billy Graham, preacher of the Gospel of Jesus Christ, went home to be with the Lord on February 21, 2018, while this manuscript was being prepared. Dr. Graham's ministry began in earnest, in conjunction with Israel's rebirth in 1948, and it continues to thrive today, seventy years later, even as the witness generation begins its final two decades and Israel celebrates its seventieth anniversary. Until recently, it was not thought possible for anyone to achieve what Billy Graham accomplished prior to the latter days. Thanks to the technology of modern travel,

Billy Graham was able to "run to and fro" (Daniel 12:4) throughout this world and preach the Gospel of Jesus Christ, witnessing to more than 200 million people in 135 nations and provinces in these latter days. He was a true shining light who fulfilled Christ's call to "preach the Gospel to all the nations" (Mark 16:15) in this rapidly darkening world. At Dr. Graham's memorial service, his daughter, Anne Graham Lotz, shared the Rapture passage (1 Thessalonians 4:13–18), and she sounded a wake-up call for Christ's pending return before a national and global TV audience with these words: "Wake up, Anne! Wake up, America! Wake up, world! Jesus is coming again! Jesus is coming soon!"[1] As a "watchman for Christ" (Ezekiel 33:1–6) and in consideration of what is revealed herein, I can only echo Anne's words: "Wake up, world! Jesus is coming! Jesus is coming soon! Perhaps today!"

Are you ready?

APPENDIX 1

SCRIPTURAL SUPPORT FOR THE CREATION NARRATIVE

The Old and New Testaments are clear and consistent in their affirmation of the Bible's Creation narrative. The words of God confirmed it (Exodus 20:11), God's finger etched it in stone (Exodus 31:18), Jesus Christ reaffirmed it (Matthew 19:4; Mark 10:5–7), and Scripture reveals that Jesus Christ is not only our Savior and Redeemer, but He is also our Creator (John 1:1–3). The purpose of this appendix is to highlight Old and New Testament passages that confirm and expand on the Bible's creation narrative. In the passages listed below, the italicized words and phrases are commented on by "the father of the modern creation movement," the late Dr. Henry Morris. His comments and notes are cited from *The New Defenders Study Bible*. It is hoped that these passages increase knowledge and faith in the only true account of origins: the creation narrative in Genesis 1 of God's holy Word.

Old Testament Confirmations

In giving Moses the Ten Commandments, God said this:

God spake all these words saying (Exodus 20:1)

Six days shalt thou labor, and do all thy work. But
the seventh day is the Sabbath of the Lord thy
God ... For *in six days* the Lord made heaven and
earth, the sea, and *all that in them is*, and rested on
the seventh day. (Exodus 20:9–11)

Dr. Morris comments on the italicized portions of this Scripture
passage and those that follow.

> **"in six days.** This verse, written on stone by God's
> own hand (Ex 31:18) settles once and for all the
> question of the meaning of 'day' in the creation
> chapter (Ge 1)... God's week was of precisely the
> same duration and pattern as man's regular week.
> The Hebrew word for days (*yamim*), furthermore,
> is used more than 700 times in the Old Testament,
> and cannot be shown ever to require any meaning
> except that of literal days, and never to anything
> comparable to geological ages... Still further, 'all
> that in them is' was made in six days; nothing had
> been made previously, as the gap theory of Genesis
> would require. There seems to be no legitimate
> interpretation of Genesis that can ever allow for
> the theoretical ages of evolutionary geology..."[1]

Another Old Testament confirmation of the Genesis 1 Creation
account is found in Psalm 33. The NLT version is given first,
followed by the KJV, with Dr. Morris's comments on the KJV.

The Lord merely spoke and the heavens were created. He breathed the word, and all the stars were born. He assigned the sea its boundaries and locked the oceans in vast reservoirs … For when he spoke, the world began! It appeared at his command. (Psalm 33:6–7, 9 NLT)[2]

By the word of the Lord were the heavens made, and all the host of them by the *breadth of his mouth*. He gathered the waters of the sea together as a heap… For he spake, and *it was done*; he commanded and it stood fast. (Psalm 33:6–7, 9 KJV)

"Breadth of his mouth"—The vast spaces of the cosmos, with all their innumerable stars and galaxies, were called into existence by the omnipotent Word of Christ (Jo 1:3). God did not use processes of stellar evolution for this purpose. If such processes could account for the universe, God would be redundant. The Genesis account records 17 occasions of God speaking "it was done." God did not take billions of years to accomplish His work of creation. There is no "process" of creation; each creative act was an instantaneous event not explainable by natural processes.[3]

New Testament Confirmations

There is compelling evidence in the New Testament that not only confirms the Creation narrative in Genesis but reveals Christ's role in it. John 1:1–4 is a foundational creation passage. From Scripture and the notes that follow, Jesus Christ is the Word, and so His name is added in parentheses after *Word* in the passage.

In the beginning was the *Word* [Jesus Christ], and the Word [Jesus Christ] was with God, and *the*

Word [Jesus Christ] *was God*. The same was in the beginning with God. All things were *made by him* [Jesus Christ], and without him [Jesus Christ] was not anything made that was made. In him [Jesus Christ] was life; and the life was the light of men. (John 1:1–4)

Dr. Morris provides much illumination about these verses.

"**In the beginning**"—It is significant that the apostle John began his Gospel with the words "in the beginning." He obviously intended that his record should start with the same words in Genesis, that is, with creation. His explicit purpose in writing was to win the readers to Christ as Son of God and Savior (see 20:30–31), and he realized the foundational importance of belief in special creation of all things by God. "**Word**"—The "Word" (Greek *logos)* is the first of at least a dozen titles given to Christ in this first chapter of John's Gospel… Probably, "the Word of God," a phrase used more than 1,200 times in the Old Testament, is the most meaningful.

"**The Word was God**"—This is a very strong assertion that Jesus is God. The eternal Word, who was to be made man (1:14), is God (not merely "a god" as some have alleged), and is the same God who created heaven and earth in the beginning. In fact, He is the only 'true God (1 Jo 5:20) who was there "in the beginning."

"**Made by him**"—This is an emphatic statement declaring that Jesus Christ, before His incarnation, had made everything in the universe. He is the God of Genesis 1:1, the God of all creation. Furthermore, note that "all things were made.' They are *not now* being made, as the concept of evolution requires. The Creator rested from all his work of creating and making all things (Ge 2:1–3) after six days of the creation week. Also, note the past tense in such passages as Colossians 1:16, Hebrews 1:2–3, and other verses dealing with creation.[4]

In both Matthew's and Mark's versions of this New Testament passage, Jesus Himself affirms the creation account.

> And the Pharisees came to him, and asked him, Is it lawful for a man to put away his wife? tempting him … And Jesus answered and said unto them *"Have you not read …"* (Matthew 19:4)

> But *from the beginning of the creation* God made them male and female. For this cause shall a man leave his father and mother, and cleave to his wife. (Mark 10:2, 5–7)

Dr. Morris's notes are as follows.

> **"Have you not read …?"**—The Lord quotes the account of the creation in Genesis as His authority in response to a vital question about the most important of all human institutions (marriage and family). It is obvious that, contrary to the popular opinion of modern intellectuals and liberal theologians, He regarded the creation record as historically true and divinely inspired.[5]

> **"The beginning of the creation"**—Mark's account adds important additional information that the Genesis record from which he is quoting referred to "the beginning of the creation." That is, God made Adam and Eve (Ge 1:26–27) right at the

very beginning—not some 4.5 billion years after the beginning, as modern evolutionists would have us believe ... There is no room whatsoever in Scripture for the geological ages and Christians who compromise on this issue for the sake of academic acceptance are undermining God's Word.[6]

The apostle Paul probably wrote more about the tragic consequences for those throughout history who have and will reject the Creation and the Creator than any New Testament writer. And he did it using very strong language. This is what Paul says in his letter to the Romans.

For the invisible things of him *from the creation* of the world are clearly seen, being understood by the things that are made, even *his eternal power* and Godhead; so that they are *without excuse.* Because that, *when they knew God*, they glorified him not as God, neither were thankful; but became vain in their imaginations and their foolish heart was darkened. Professing themselves to be wise, *they became fools*, and changed the glory of the uncorruptible God into an image made like to corruptible man, and to birds, and four footed creatures, and creeping things... Who changed the truth of God into a lie, and worshipped and served the *creature more than the Creator*, who blessed them forever. Amen. (Romans 1:20–23, 25)

Dr. Morris's notes follow.

"From the creation"—That is, from the very time of creation, men should have seen the evidence of God's existence and His work in the marvelous universe which He had created for "God hath shewed it unto them" (1:19). "The heavens declare

92

the glory of God, and the firmament sheweth His handywork" (Ps 19:1). These things should have been seen and understood by men from the very time of the creation of the world, so it is clear that the creation did not take place billions of years before men appeared on earth as evolutionists and progressive creationists have alleged.[7]

"His eternal power"—It is God's eternal power which is evident in the cosmos, the power which created it, not just the power which sustains it once it has been created. The remarkable significance of this fact is illuminated by the modern discovery of the two most important and universal laws of science, known technically as the first and second laws of thermodynamics. More popularly, they can be understood, respectively, as the law of conservation of the quantity of all things God created (energy), and the law of deterioration in the "organized complexity" of all things God created. The first law reflects the completion of creation in the past (Ge 2:1–3), so that nothing is now being either created or annihilated; creation is being conserved. The second law reflects the subsequent curse on creation because of sin (8:20–22, Ge 3:17–19), so that everything now has a strong tendency to die—that is to disintegrate back to dust (the basic elements), from which he made all the complex systems in the cosmos.[8]

"Without excuse"—The phrase "without excuse" is, literally "without an apologetic" or "without a defense." First Peter 3:15 instructs Christians to "be ready always to give an answer." In other words, Christians do have an apologetic and ought to be ready to give it whenever someone attacks or questions their faith. Those who do not see the eternal power and nature of God in the creation… have no apologetic. They are "without excuse" if they do not believe in our Creator God. The evidence is all around them.[9]

"When they knew God"—Romans 1:21–28 describes the awful descent of the ancient world from their ancestral knowledge of the true God, as received from Father Noah, down into evolutionary pantheism and its accompanying polytheism (1:21–25) and then into the gross immorality and wickedness that inevitably follows such apostasy.

"They became fools"—Those who deny the God of creation are fools (Ps 14:1) and without a defense. Yet they come to such a foolish decision in the foolish belief that they are scientific in trying to explain the infinitely complex, majestic, beautiful creation without a Creator. The ancient pagans did this with immeasurably tragic results … Modern evangelicals are in serious danger of starting down that same slippery slope, compromising with evolutionism and increasingly flirting with New Age pantheism, feminism, and occultism (compare 2 Timothy 3:1–13).[10]

"Creature more than the Creator"—The ancient pagans originally knew the true God but in only a few generations after the flood, under the leadership of Nimrod (Ge 10:8–11; 11:1–9) they rebelled against Him and proceeded to worship the forces and systems of nature instead of the God who had created all these things, assuming either that the cosmos had always existed or else that it had somehow evolved itself from primordial chaos.[11]

Paul saves some of his strongest language for the rejecters of creationism—the evolutionary humanists of the latter days—in his letters to Timothy. His words are important because they reflect the natural tendency of the human mindset that will prevail in the latter days. Today, we are in the latter days, as the Bible-based chronology reveals in chapter 6, when the issue of origins is more divisive than ever.

> This know also, that in the last days *perilous times* shall come. For men shall be *lovers of their own selves,* covetous, boasters, proud, blasphemers, disobedient to parents, unthankful, unholy, *without natural affection*, trucebreakers, false accusers, incontinent, fierce, despisers of those that are good. Traitors, heady, highminded, lovers of pleasures more than lovers of God; having a form of godliness but *denying the power* thereof … *Ever learning*, and never able to come to the knowledge of the truth. (2 Timothy 3:1–5, 7)

Dr. Morris's notes:

> **"Perilous times"**—"Perilous" could also be translated "fierce" or "furious" … The world will become increasingly violent and dangerous as the end approaches.

> **"Lovers of their own selves"**—This catalog of the dangerous last days begins with what is essentially a definition of modern humanists: "lovers of their own selves." The entire list seems peculiarly descriptive of the emphasis and attributes of modern evolutionary humanism … except that the characteristics listed here in Paul's letter to Timothy seem to be developing within the framework of the

95

professing church rather than the pagan world. In other words, there will be little distinction between the secular world and the religious world in the last days. Note in particular the cult of self-love, now being strongly promoted by secular psychologists and increasingly prominent in counseling methods used in modern evangelical churches, as the answer to all psychological and sociological problems.

"Without natural affection"—Evidently a great and dangerous increase in perverse sexual behavior will characterize the last days. The descent into evolutionary paganism is always followed by gross immorality, specifically including sexual perversion, such as described in Romans 1:26–29 … Ancient Sodom was so notorious for homosexuality that its practice has long been known as sodomy. The practice became so widespread in ancient Greece that it was considered normal and even desirable. Other examples are abundant and, of course, it is quickly becoming accepted—even encouraged—here in America. Not surprisingly, this was preceded by widespread return to evolutionism in science and education.[12]

"Denying the power"—These latter day humanists will have a pseudo-religion, but will deny its power— that is, its supernatural aspects (creation, miracles, second coming, heaven, hell, regeneration). This description would apply specifically to religious humanists, to the liberal theologians who dominate the mainline denominations, to modernists, and to most New Age cultists.

"Ever learning"—This is the precise emphasis of modern "intellectual" educators. They say there is no absolute truth. They also contend that we must continually be searching for truth, but can never really find ultimate truth and should never make such a claim.[13]

Paul's fifth charge in his letters to Timothy appropriately addresses the issue of "false science," and it is expounded on as evolutionism by Dr. Morris.

> O Timothy, keep that which is committed to thy trust, avoiding profane and vain babblings, and oppositions of *science falsely so called*. (1 Timothy 6:20)

> **"Science falsely so called"**—"Science falsely so called" is, literally "pseudo-science" or "pseudo-knowledge" in the Greek. This pseudo-science is nothing other than evolutionism which has been in "oppositions" against God as Savior and Creator, and against the world as His creation, since the beginning of time. In Paul's day, it mainly took the form of Epicureanism (based on atheistic evolutionism) and Stoicism (based on pantheistic evolutionism). It soon would take the form of Gnosticism and later of Neo-Platonism, both assuming evolution. In recent times it assumed the form of Darwinism, though men are now returning again to various forms of eastern religion and their systems of pantheistic evolution, still rejecting God as Creator and Christ as Savior. Yet all forms of evolutionism are pseudo-science at best, filled with "profane and vain babblings." Note the following summary of current scientific evidence against evolutionism.

1. There is no present evolution, only horizontal variations and extinctions.
2. There was no past evolution, only gaps between basic kinds in fossils.
3. There can be no possible evolution, since universal laws of conservation and decay now govern all natural processes.
4. There has been no time period long enough for evolution, because historical records go back only a few thousand years, and the fossil record speaks only of rapid formation.
5. There is no biblical evolution (see Ge 1:25; 2:1–3; 1 Cor 15:38–39).
6. There can have been no theistic evolution, for death came into the world only when man sinned (Ro 5:12; 1 Cor 15:21).
7. There could have been no pantheistic evolution, for God condemns all who worship the creation as its own creator (Ro 1:20–25).[14]

In closing, the words from Dr. Morris's commentary on *The Logic of Biblical Creation* are most appropriate.

The biblical account of creation is ridiculed by atheists, patronized by liberals, and often allegorized even by conservatives. The fact is, however, that it is God's own account of creation, corroborated by Jesus Christ (Mk 10:6–8) who was there. We are well advised to take it seriously and literally, for God is able to say what He means and someday will hold us accountable for believing *(or not believing)* what He says. Furthermore, the account is reasonable and logical, fully in accord with all true science and history.[15]

APPENDIX 2

HEBREW/GREGORIAN CALENDAR DATES FOR PASSOVER AND EASTER, 2001–2021

Year	Passover Date[1]	Year Length	Easter Date	Year Length	Pass/East Difference
5781/2021	March 28–29	355 days	April 4	357 days	7 days
5780/2020	April 9–10	355 days	April 12	356 days	3 days
5779/2019	April 20–21	**385** days	April 21	385 days	0 days
5778/2018	Mar 31–April 1	355 days	April 1	350 days	0 days
5777/2017	April 11–12	353 days	April 16	385 days	5 days
5776/2016	April 23–24	**384** days	March 27	356 days	27 days
5775/2015	April 4–5	354 days	April 20	385 days	5 days
5774/2014	April 15–16	**385** days	April 20	385 days	5 days
5773/2013	March 26–27	353 days	March 31	356 days	4 days
5772/2012	April 7–8	353 days	April 8	353 days	0 days
5771/2011	April 19–20	**385** days	April 24	385 days	5 days
5770/2010	March 30–31	355 days	April 4	357 days	5 days
5769/2009	April 9–10	354 days	April 12	385 days	3 days
5768/2008	April 20–21	**382** days	March 23	349 days	28 days
5767/2007	April 3–4	355 days	April 8	357 days	5 days
5766/2006	April 13–14	354 days	April 16	385 days	3 days

5765/2005	April 24–25	**383** days	March 27	350 days	28 days
5764/2004	April 6–7	354 days	April 11	356 days	5 days
5763/2003	April 17–18	**385** days	April 20	385 days	3 days
5762/2002	March 28–29	354 days	March 31	350 days	3 days
5761/2001	April 8–9	353 days	April 15	357 days	7 days

The contemporary Hebrew calendar above (2021–2001) is reckoned much like it was by the ancient Hebrews. It is based on the lunar cycle (29 1/2 days per month) and is defined as twelve thirty-day months, or a 360-day year. Because the solar calendar contains 365 1/4 days and the lunar calendar contains only 354 days, the eleven day difference is resolved by the addition of a thirteenth month (called an intercalary month) to reckon the lunar calendar with the solar year. Lunar calendar reckoning requires seven intercalations every nineteen years. The years in bold print above (382–385 days in length) reflect the seven intercalations required during the current twenty-year period. The Hebrew calendar is calculated to begin on 1 Nisan (Sacred New Year), and so the Passover always occurs on the fourteenth day of Nisan during the first (or rare second) full moon (March–April) after the vernal equinox. The Jewish civil New Year begins on 1 Tishri despite the year being reckoned annually on 1 Nisan. Easter, shown in the right columns, is celebrated on the first Sunday after the first full moon following the vernal equinox each year. There are no 360-day years in either calendar based on the Passover and Easter holidays.

APPENDIX 3

WAS THE CRUCIFIXION PASSOVER ON APRIL 2 OR APRIL 3, 33 AD?

In chapter 4, I indicate that my 2013 Christmas star research revealed the date for Christ's crucifixion to be April 3, 33 AD, which was in agreement with Ussher and other historians. Using the Starry Night astronomy software, I had confirmed the moon was full throughout the night of Friday, April 3, and so believed the Passover began on Friday evening at sunset. But on March 29, 2018, in his Resurrection Sunday program on the *Hal Lindsey Report*, Hal Lindsey revealed an important verse in Scripture that I had not considered. In responding to the Scribes' and Pharisees' request to show them a sign, Jesus said that the only sign they would see was the sign of Jonah: "Just as Jonah spent three days and three nights in the belly of the great fish, so will the Son of man spend three days and three nights in the heart of the earth" (Matthew 12:40). The three nights Jesus spoke of in this passage got my attention because a crucifixion on Friday (April 3) provides for only two nights if the resurrection was on Sunday morning (the first day of the week), which Scripture confirms that it was.

I previously confirmed the moon was a full moon on the night of April 3 but decided to take another look at the moon for that Passover on my astronomy software. The camera was set in Jerusalem to confirm that it was the same moon that the Jews would have observed. What I discovered was interesting. When the moon rose on Thursday evening, April 2, it was waxing-gibbous and 13.89 days old (looked like a full moon). The moon remained waxing gibbous until it became full at 4:34 a.m. (one hour twenty minutes before sunrise) on the morning of April 3. The moon remained full until it set at 6:17 a.m. on the morning of April 4. If the Passover began at sunset on April 3, as has been assumed, the moon had been a full moon for about fourteen hours before the Passover began, and so Jesus would have been crucified and died while the moon was already full.

Depending on how the Jews reckoned the new moon and the start of Passover, I thought it at least plausible, based on what I'd observed, for the Passover to start on Thursday evening, April 2. If true and Christ was crucified on Thursday, then it would support the three nights (Thursday, Friday, and Saturday) required to fulfill Scripture (Matthew 12:40). I sent this information to astronomer Dr. Danny Faulkner (*Answers in Genesis* astronomer) who responded quickly with the following.

> There was a partial lunar eclipse the evening of April 3. Mid-eclipse was about a half hour before the moon rose over Jerusalem on April 3. Mid-eclipse must coincide with astronomical full moon, so the time of full moon would have been about 5:30 PM on April 3, not 4:33 AM the morning of April 3, 13 hours earlier.

I confirmed the eclipse on the NASA lunar eclipse page. Then I checked the eclipse on my astronomy software from Jerusalem. The moon rose on the evening of April 3 in Jerusalem at 8:15 p.m., and so mid-eclipse would have been nearly three hours earlier. The eclipse was over by 6:30 p.m., almost two hours before moonrise.

The moon would have been observed as a full moon to those in Jerusalem, both when it set on the morning of April 3 and when it rose that same evening. Modern technology lets us know when there is a lunar eclipse, but I'm not sure how anyone in Israel at the time would have known there was a lunar eclipse that day because it would not have been observed in Jerusalem.

I then decided to see when the new moon appeared to mark 1 Nisan for the AD 33 Passover. On the astronomy software, the moon changed from waxing to new at 4:08 a.m. on March 19. The new moon is too close to the sun to be seen during daylight and so would not have been observed as a new moon by anyone on the ground before sunset on March 19. This is when it was first possible for the "two Jewish witnesses" to observe the new moon and report it to the temple priests during the temple period. If true, and the observance at sunset on March 19 marked March 19–20 as 1 Nisan, then fourteen days later was April 1–2. If the witnesses reported the new moon observance the next day, marking March 20–21 as 1 Nisan, then fourteen days later was April 2–3. Based on a new moon sighting on March 19 or 20, the Passover would most likely have been established to be either April 1 or 2 as opposed to April 3, which was either fifteen or sixteen days after the 1 Nisan date.

Although the new moon appearance on March 19–21 seems to support the case for a 2 April Passover, I decided to check the modern calendar to see how the times for the full moon appearance matched with the calendar dates for the Passover and compare them with times and dates for the Exodus Passover and the AD 33 Passover. The table below shows the results. A plus sign in the right column means the full moon appeared that number of hours before the calendar start of the Passover. A minus sign in the right column means the calendar start of the Passover began that many hours before the full moon appeared during the Passover. As the table shows, all the modern calendar Passovers, except 2013, occur after the full moon appears, some by as much as two days.

Start of Full Moon on Passover (Observed from Jerusalem)

Date	Passover Date	Full Moon Date	Full Moon Time	Hrs +/- Passover Start
Exodus 1446 BC	April 23–24	April 23–24	12:08 a.m. Ap 24 – 12:32 a.m. Ap 25	-5 hours
1446 BC	March 25–26	March 25–26	10:16 a.m. Ma 25 – 12:06 p.m. Ma 26	+9:15 hours
Passion 33 AD	April 02–03	April 3–4	5:34 a.m. Apr 3 – 7:47 a.m. Apr 4	-10 hours
33 AD	April 03–04	April 3–4	5:34 a.m. Apr 3 – 7:47 a.m. Apr 4	+13:45 hours
5760/2000	April 20–21	April 18–19	9:27 a.m. Apr 18 – 10:04 a.m. Apr 19	+58 hours
5761/2001	April 8–9	April 7–8	8:28 p.m. April 7 – 6:23 p.m. April 8	+25 hours
5762/2002	March 28–29	March 28–29	12:08 p.m. Mar 28 – 8:40 a.m. Mar 29	+6:50 hours
5763/2003	April 17–18	April 16–17	1:21 p.m. Apr 16 – 9:52 a.m. Apr 17	+30 hours
5764/2004	April 6–7	April 5–6	4:01 a.m. April 5 – 2:02 a.m. April 6	+39 hours
5765/2005	April 24–25	April 24–25	2:26 a.m. Apr 24 – 1:41 a.m. Apr 25	+16:34 hours
5766/2006	April 13–14	April 13–14	7:37 a.m. Apr 13 – 9:36 a.m. Apr 14	+12 hours
5767/2007	April 3–4	April 2–3	7:46 a.m. April 2 – 10:46 a.m. April 3	+36:15 hours
5768/2008	April 20–21	April 20–21	1:17 a.m. Apr 20 – 3:38 a.m. Apr 21	+19 hours
5769/2009	April 9–10	April 9–10	7:04 a.m. April 9 – 6:55 a.m. April 10	+12:20 hours
5770/2010	March 30–31	March 29–30	7:50 p.m. Mar 29 – 5:08 p.m. Mar 30	+24:30 hours
5771/2011	April 19–20	April 17–18	8:27 p.m. Apr 17 – 5:04 p.m. Apr 18	+47 hours
5772/2012	April 7–8	April 6–7	12:56 p.m. Apr 6 – 9:39 a.m. Apr 7	+31 hours

5773/2013	March 26–27	March 27–28	2:05 a.m. Mar 27– 12:44 a.m. Mar 28	- 6:30 hours
5774/2014	April 15–16	April 14–15	11:36 p.m. Apr 14 – 11:42 p.m. Apr 15	+21:36 hours
5775/2015	April 4–5	April 4–5	2:47 a.m. Apr 4 – 5:21 a.m. Apr 5	+16:45 hours
5777/2017	April 11–12	April 10–11	9:18 p.m. Apr 10– 11:07 p.m. Apr 11	+21:30 hours
5778/2018	Mar 31–Apr 1	Mar 31– Apr 1	5:08 a.m. Mar 31 – 4:14 a.m. Apr 1	+14:27 hours
5779/2019	April 20–21	April 18–19	4:23 a.m. Apr 19 – 9:50 p.m. Apr 20	+37 hours
5780/2020	April 9–10	April 7–8	8:25 p.m. Apr 7 – 10:13 p.m. Apr 8	+49 hours

Because I don't know how the modern Hebrew calendar Passover dates are determined, or what location the dates are determined from (if there is a specific location), it is difficult to know how useful the modern calendar data are. What I found to be interesting relates to the two possible dates for the Exodus Passover. The year 1446 BC had two possible Passover dates, one in March (after the vernal equinox) and one in April. As can be seen from Appendix 1 and in the table above, it is rare, if ever, that a Passover is celebrated before March 26. This is because the appearance of a full moon between March 21–22 and March 26 affords a convenient opportunity to add an intercalary month to the Jewish calendar—something that is necessary every two or three years. Thus, it is highly likely that the Exodus Passover was on April 23–24, 1446 BC. What is significant about this date is that God told Moses the angel of death would appear at midnight (Exodus 12:29) to smite all the firstborn throughout the land who were not a part of the Passover. In 1446 BC, if the Passover began at sunset on April 23, then less than five hours later, at 12:08 a.m. (essentially midnight), the moon became full. This timing makes a strong case for the Passover starting at sunset before the moon becomes full, and so it adds support for a April 2, 33 AD, Passover date for the crucifixion.

From this evidence, a case can be made for a Thursday, April 2,

33 AD, crucifixion and Passover start that fulfills Matthew 12:40. That said, it is left to the reader to evaluate the data and make his or her own decision. The tables in chapters 5 and 6 show a April 2–3 Passover date for Jesus's crucifixion that fits in either case.

References

Preface

1   Henry M. Morris, *The New Defenders Study Bible (KJV)*, (1995 by World Publishing), Introduction, p. v

Chapter 1- Biblical Chronology of the Patriarchs from the Creation to Jacob

1   Henry M. Morris, *The New Defenders Study Bible (KJV)*, (1995 by World Publishing), Appendix 10, p. 2097

Chapter 3 - Biblical Chronology for the Period of the Hebrew Kings and the Establishment of an Absolute Date linking Two Halves of Bible History

1   Edwin R. Thiele, *Mysterious Numbers of the Hebrew Kings* (3rd Edition, Anguin, CA 1982, Copyright: The Zondervan Corporation, 1983)
2   Thiele, Chapter 4, p. 68
3   Thiele, Chapter 5, p. 79
4   Thiele, List of Dates for Rulers of Judah and Israel pp.10-11
5   Thiele, Appendix G Note, p. 228
6   Thiele, Appendix G List of the Rulers of Persia, pp. 227-228
7   James Ussher, *Annals of the World*, (Revised and updated by Larry & Marion Pierce, 2006, Master Books), Appendix G pp. 932-933
8   Ussher, The Epistle to the Reader, p. 9, The Annals of the Old Testament, p. 17

9   Henry M. Morris, *The New Defenders Study Bible (KJV)*, (1995 by World Publishing), Note on Genesis 11:32, p. 54

10 Morris, Note on Ezra 3:1, p. 711

11 Thiele, Chapter 2, p. 53

Chapter 4 - The Period between the Decree of Artaxerxes and the Incarnate Jesus Christ

1   Sir Robert Anderson, *The Coming Prince (1896)*, Reprinted in 1957 from the tenth edition published by Kregel Classics, Chapter 10 pp. 127-128

2   Anderson, Chapter 6, p. 70

3   Ibid., p.71

4   Ibid., pp. 74-75

5   Grant Jeffrey, *The 360 Day Prophetic Year in the Bible*, http://xwalk.ca/360day.html

6   Anderson, Chapter 6, p. 67

7   Edwin R. Thiele, *Mysterious Numbers of the Hebrew Kings* (3rd Edition, Anguin, CA 1982, Copyright: The Zondervan Corporation, 1983), Chapter 4, p. 67

8   Anderson, Appendix 2, p. 258

9   Anderson, Chapter 6, p. 70

10 Ibid., p. 71

11 Ibid., pp. 74-75

12 Anderson, Chapter 10 pp. 127-128

13 James Ussher, *Annals of the World*, (Revised and updated by Larry & Marion Pierce, 2006, Master Books), Vol. 2 – The Seventh Age of the World, p. 822

Chapter 5 - A Chronology for the Incarnate Christ: The Heavens Declare the Glory of God

1   The Holy Bible, *New International Version* (The Zondervan Corporation, 1990), Psalm 19:1-3, pp. 842-843

2   Henry M. Morris, *The New Defenders Study Bible (KJV)*, (1995 by World Publishing), Note on Numbers 24:17, p. 281

3   Morris, Note on Revelation 22:16, p. 2045

4   Jim Dodge, *Statistical Analysis of 200 Years of Venus Jupiter Conjunctions*, 2015, http://thechristmasstar.org/wp-content/uploads/2015/ StatisticalAnalysisOf200YearsOfVenus.pdf

5   Dodge, *Statistical Analysis of 9400 Years of Venus Jupiter Conjunctions*, 2015, http://the christmasstar.org/wp-content/uploads/2015/ StatisticalAnalysis9400YearsVenusJupiterConjunctions.pdf

6   Dodge, *The Sign of Revelation 12*, htttp://thechristmasstar.org/wp-content/uploads/2017/07/TheSignofRevelation12.pdf.

7   James Ussher, *Annals of the World*, (Revised and updated by Larry & Marion Pierce, 2006, Master Books), Vol. 2 The First Year of Christ's Ministry, p. 805

8   Ibid., The Second Year of Christ's Ministry, p. 806

9   Ibid., The Third Year of Christ's Ministry, p. 808

10 Ibid, The Passion Week- Palm Sunday, p.813

11 Ibid., The Passion Week – the Crucifixion, p. 815

12 Jim Dodge, *Starry Night Pro Image – The Christmas Star over Jerusalem 17 June, 2 BC* (The Christmas Star DVD, copyright 2014)

13 Dodge, *Starry Night Pro Image – Venus over Jerusalem 17 June 2023 AD* (The Christmas Star DVD, copyright 2014)

Chapter 6 - A Bible-Based Chronology for the Second Advent of Jesus Christ

1   Henry M. Morris, *The New Defenders Study Bible (KJV)*, (1995 by World Publishing), p. 1438

2   The Holy Bible, *New International Version* (The Zondervan Corporation, 1990), p.1292

3   Ibid., p.1159

4   Brent Miller Jr., *The Coming Convergence DVD* (Ingenuity Films LLC, 2017), Chapter 4

5   Morris, Note on Psalm 90:10, p. 901

6   U.S. Census Data – 2016 (https://www.census.gov/programs-surveys/ popest/data/data-sets.2016.html)

7   Morris, Note on Revelation 3:10, p. 1993

8   Gary Stearman, *Ask Gary Stearman*, (Prophecy Watcher Magazine, March 2018), p. 11

9   The Barna Group (www.barna.com) Christian Worldview Analysis (2001)

Conclusion

1   Anne Graham Lotz remarks, *Fox News coverage of Billy Graham Funeral service,* March 2, 2018

Appendix 1

1   Henry M. Morris, *The New Defenders Study Bible (KJV),* (1995 by World Publishing), Notes on Ex 20:11, pp. 158-159

2   *Holy Bible,* New Living Translation, Copyright 1996 by the Tyndall House Foundation, Psalm 33:6-7, 9

3   Morris, Notes on Psalm 33:6-7, 9, p. 853

4   Morris, Notes on John 1:1-4, p.1563

5   Morris, Note on Matthew 19:4, p.1427

6   Morris, Note on Mark 10:6, p. 1476

7   Morris, Note on Romans 1:20, pp.1699-1700

8   Ibid., p. 1700

9   Ibid., p. 1701

10   Morris, Notes on Romans 1:21,22, p. 1701

11   Morris, Note on Romans 1:25, p. 1701-1702

12   Morris, Notes on 2 Timothy 3:1-5, pp. 1875-1876

13   Morris, Note on 2 Timothy 3:7, p. 1876

14   Morris, Notes on 1 Timothy 6:20, p. 1869

15   Morris, Commentary on *The Logic of Biblical Creation,* Appendix 3, p. 2067

Appendix 2

1   Hebrew Calendar, *Passover dates,*(https://www.hebcal.com/holidays/)

Appendix 3

1   New Moon/Full Moon times from Jerusalem, *Starry Night Pro Astronomy software,* @ Simulation Curriculum Corporation, 2009

CPSIA information can be obtained
at www.ICGtesting.com
Printed in the USA
LVHW041058170319
610949LV00001B/309/P